BEARS

· WILD GUIDE ·

BEARS

Charles Fergus

illustrations by Amelia Hansen

STACKPOLE
BOOKS

Published by
STACKPOLE BOOKS
5067 Ritter Road
Mechanicsburg, PA 17055
www.stackpolebooks.com

Printed in China

10 9 8 7 6 5 4 3 2 1

First edition

Cover design by Caroline Stover
Illustrations by Amelia Hansen
Photo credits: JessLeePhotos.com: 8, 18, 19, 23, 25, 28, 44, 50, 60, 70, 87, 93, 94, 112;
Gerry Lemmo: 33, 37, 49, 68, 104, 106; Len Rue Jr.: 41; Mark Elbroch: 79

Library of Congress Cataloging-in-Publication Data

Fergus, Charles.
    Bears / Charles Fergus ; illustrations by Amelia Hansen.— 1st ed.
      p.   cm. — (Wild guide)
    Includes bibliographical references.
    ISBN-13: 978-0-8117-3251-2
    ISBN-10: 0-8117-3251-7
    1. Black bear. I. Hansen, Amelia. II. Title. III. Series.
QL737.C27F47 2005
599.78'5—dc22
                                           2005014204

CONTENTS

INTRODUCTION

Bears project a mighty physical presence and a capacity for action. They are smart, something that often becomes apparent the moment you come face-to-face with one. Bears, with their great size and strength, remind us of how weak and ineffectual we are as organisms: a bear, even a small one, could abolish a human fairly easily. It is our good fortune that bears are generally circumspect around us, because hunters have taught them, over millennia, to respect our own capabilities, technologically and socially enhanced though they may be.

Bears remind us of ourselves. They walk on the flats of their feet, as people do. They may stand up on their hind feet or sit down on their rumps. The carcass of a skinned bear is said to show an uncanny resemblance to the human body. Many native peoples attribute human characteristics to bears, including wisdom and courage. Bears figure prominently in legend and myth, and have been identified in the constellations of the night sky by a host of cultures. People probably have revered bears for as long as we have interacted with them. And while bear worship is not a part of most modern religions, it is natural for us—even those of us who have never seen a bear—to be awed by such magnificent and formidable creatures.

Although more than thirty years have passed, I can still remember the first wild bear I ever saw. The bear stood on a grassy hillside in northern Pennsylvania. I was with three other hikers, and we stopped and drank in the sight of the bear. It was a big one, and its coat reflected in bright waves and winks the sun that came filtering through the leaves of the trees. The bear was so black that it seemed to gather all the light in the forest unto itself. It gathered our attention completely. We watched the bear for half an hour, and although it lifted its head every now and then and glanced in our direction, it was clearly more interested in eating grass than in looking at people.

Half an hour later, I spotted bears number two through six of my incipient bear-sighting career: a female and four cubs, about 50 yards away. The cubs were the size of cocker spaniels; the sow was the size of a Great Dane, but she looked bigger than that, especially when she turned her broad head and stared at us. Unlike bear number one, these bears were on the same side of the stream as the trail we were following. The sow's rounded ears stood erect. Her nose wrinkled as she tested the air for scent. We heard a sound like glass being trodden on, and breaking and grating underfoot: a warning delivered by bear teeth. Suddenly the sow gave out with an explosive, doglike *woof*, and her cubs began ambling away. The sow turned and, in a quick, limber walk, followed the cubs down the trail.

Ian Frazier has written, "A woods with a bear in it is real to a man walking through it in a way that a woods with no bear is not."

Since that day in the early 1970s, bears have made the woods real to me many times. I have jotted down most of those encounters in something I whimsically labeled "Bear Scorecard."(I recommend that readers keep a similar journal to include sightings—easily found if you know what to look for—of the many signs that bears leave in nature.) Over the years, I have recorded a Wisconsin black bear, already fast asleep in mid-October, its head visible when we got down on hands and knees and peered into its recently excavated den. A dark-coated, silver-tipped grizzly chasing a herd of young elk back and forth across a high-country meadow in the Lamar Valley of Wyoming's Yellowstone National Park. A Pennsylvania black bear that, as I watched from only a few feet away, unseen and unscented, stood on its hind legs and rubbed its back up and down on a rough-barked oak. (At the time, I assumed the bear was scratching an itch; now, having studied biologists' interpretations of bear behavior, I realize the bruin was probably using the tree as a signpost.)

On a chilly autumn night in the Boundary Waters Canoe Area Wilderness in northern Minnesota, a black bear climbed the tree where we'd carefully hung our food, broke the limb from which the bags were suspended, and fell to the ground along with our three food sacks. The bear then ran off with the sack containing our breakfasts. This unwelcome visitor came back twice in the night, trying to get the rest of our food; we drove him off by shouting and throwing stones. In the morning—hoarse, exhausted, and ready to put several portages between ourselves and that ill-chosen campsite—I found one of our plastic jars about 100 feet from the tent, where the bear had gone and eaten. I still have the jar. In the rim of the lid, at about four and eight o'clock, are two holes $2^1/2$ inches apart, punched out by the bear's teeth.

This book is for people who live around bears; who enjoy walking, hiking, canoeing, fishing, or camping in areas inhabited by bears; and who simply want to learn more about bears.

At the opening of the twenty-first century, bears are becoming more numerous in some regions, including much of the eastern United States. In other parts of the world, bear numbers are dwindling. Some bears are growing more accustomed to humans—and more aware of our physical limitations. Over the last forty years, scientists have learned much about the biology and habits of bears, particularly the three species that occur in North America. It behooves us to better understand these animals. We can then protect our food from hungry bears. We can coexist with bears and protect their habitats, which in turn will preserve the habitats of many smaller creatures. And we can more fully enjoy and understand nature, and our place in it, as well as the place occupied by these splendid creatures.

1

What Makes a Bear a Bear?

Bears belong to Carnivora, the order of mammals whose members eat meat; other carnivores include dogs, raccoons, weasels, skunks, and cats. Bears are some of the most omnivorous of the carnivores, eating many vegetable foods in addition to flesh. Bears' feeding habits determine almost everything about them: their size, shape, skeleton, and musculature; the form and size of their teeth, paws, and claws; their sensory capabilities; their reproduction; their home ranges and movements across the landscape; and the cycle of their activity throughout the year.

Physical Characteristics and Senses

Bears are covered with thick fur that insulates them against heat and cold. Different kinds of bears live in a variety of environments, from steamy jungles to frozen wastes, and from open plains to deep forests. They range in size from the sun bear of Southeast Asia, whose adults weigh 60 to 145 pounds, to arctic polar bear males, which commonly tip the scales at 1,000 pounds and sometimes exceed 1,500 pounds: ten times as large as the sun bear. In general, males are larger than same-age females of a given species.

Bears are stocky and powerfully built, with muscular shoulders and legs. They use their strength to turn over stones and logs when searching for food, deliver crushing blows to prey, and excavate dens. With a flip of its paw, a polar bear can scoop a 500-pound seal out of the water. A grizzly can run down and overpower a bison or moose that outweighs it by hundreds of

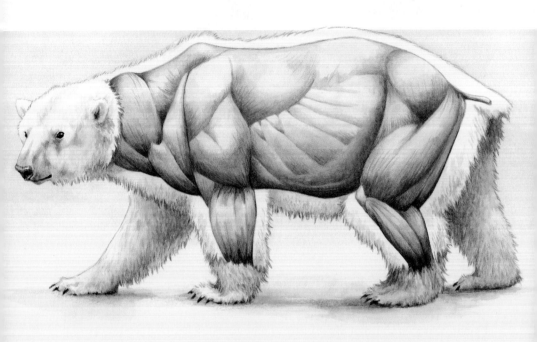

This diagram of the polar bear's musculature demonstrates why the animal is so strong.

pounds. Bears can ably defend themselves against other predators, including pumas and wolves.

People have noted a resemblance in general body shape between bears and pigs, and for this reason, male bears are often called "boars" and females "sows." Perhaps the linkage is strengthened because bears, like pigs, are big eaters that go rooting about for food on and in the ground.

Bears have short, furry tails. Mammals that are adept at jumping, such as squirrels and cats, use their long tails to keep balanced, but since a bear does not often jump, it doesn't need a long tail. Also, some biologists suggest that a bear's tail is abbreviated so that the appendage isn't constantly getting dirty from the copious amounts of food processed by the ursine digestive system.

Bears walk most of the time, although they can also trot and gallop. Should the need arise, a bear can really cover the ground: a grizzly weighing in excess of 500 pounds can quickly accelerate and hit 35 to 40 miles per hour over a short distance. But bears generally tramp along in a plantigrade fashion, placing the soles of their feet flat on the ground in the manner of raccoons and humans, rather than springing off of their toes as the faster, more cursorial (running-oriented) carnivores do. When a bear walks on all fours, its front feet turn slightly inward, reflecting the well-developed rotational capacity of its shoulders—a property that is most useful in climbing, digging, and prying. The broad hind feet act as stable platforms to let bears stand upright, the better to employ their senses and glean food from trees and shrubs. Most bears swim capably, and one species, the polar bear, often swims well out into the ocean as it moves through its territory in search of prey.

A bear has forty-two teeth. At the front of the upper and lower jaws stands a row of small incisors, bounded by a pair of sturdy, conical, slightly recurved canine teeth. Working in concert with a bear's sensitive lips, the incisors can pick up small food items such as berries and insects. The canines—up to $1^1/2$ inches long in grizzly bears—can pierce the skin of prey and drive deep into vital zones; they are also used for tearing flesh. In some carnivores, such as pumas and wolves, the carnassials, or cheek teeth, are large and sharp for shearing flesh into small, easily swallowed chunks. As bears evolved, their carnassials dwindled while their molars, or back teeth, became long, broad, relatively flat, and studded with numerous low, rounded cusps—perfect for crushing vegetation. On a bear's wide, heavy skull, prominent ridges serve as points of attachment for large muscles. These muscles move the massive jaws, providing the power that lets the molars grind plant food into digestible fragments. Bears can bite hard. Their jaws and teeth are strong enough to crack the bones of large prey animals, giving access to the nutritious marrow.

Grazers and browsers such as sheep and deer have large molars too. Their stomachs are equipped with multiple chambers and bacteria to help break down cellulose, the woody component in mature plants; those animals also ruminate, or rechew, plant matter to wring all possible nutrients out of it. Bears do not possess chambered stomachs, nor do they ruminate. They have a simple gut that, although elongated compared to that of most other carnivores, cannot digest nutritionally poor vegetation. Over the course of the year, plant foods make up more than 75 percent of the diet of most bears. In general, bears turn up their noses at old and woody growth. Instead, they select high-energy plants and plant parts, such as growing shoots, roots, bulbs, nuts, and berries. Bears feed on those foods when they are at their peak nutrient content and are easiest to digest. Since bears are large, they can pack away huge quantities of such food when it becomes available.

A bear's teeth continue to grow throughout the animal's life, adding a layer of cementum each year, much as a tree lays down an annual ring of wood. When researchers capture and anesthetize a bear, they may remove one of the animal's premolars. (The premolars barely poke through the skin between the canines and the molars, and losing one of these vestigial teeth does not seem to harm a bear in any way.) The scientists soften the tooth in acid, slice off a thin section, stain it, and examine it under a microscope. The number of rings tells the bear's age, and the width of the rings gives clues to an individual's health history and, in a female, to her years of pregnancy and lactation.

There's an old saying: "A pine needle fell in the forest. The hawk saw it, the deer heard it, and the bear smelled it." Olfaction, the ability to detect and

1.

3.

5.

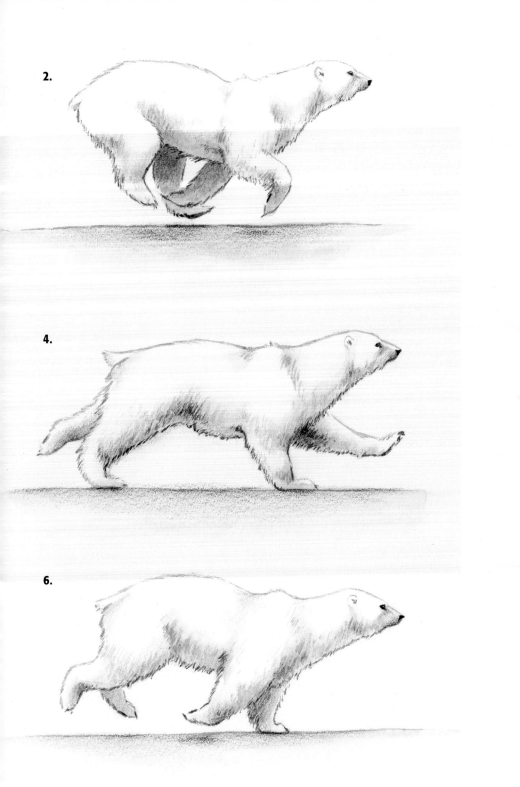

2.

4.

6.

This sequence shows a polar bear running. Bears usually get around by walking, but they can also trot and gallop. They are very fast runners over short distances.

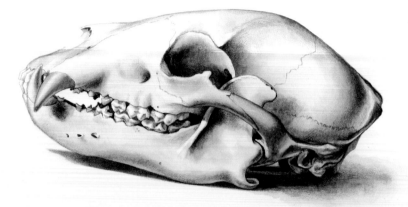

The skull and teeth of a black bear (above) are much smaller than those of a grizzly bear (below). Grizzlies have large molars for grinding up roots, bulbs, corms, and tubers. Both species use their pointed canine teeth to kill prey and for tearing flesh.

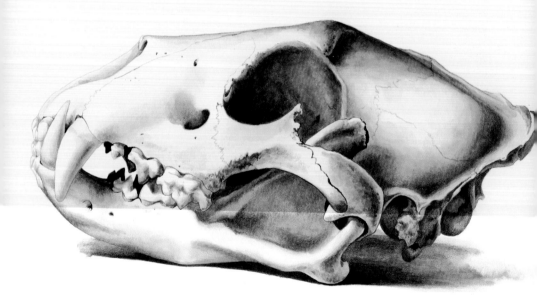

discriminate among odors, is a bear's keenest sense. A polar bear can smell a seal in a den several feet below the snow's surface; above the snow, it can locate a seal by smell from more than 20 miles away. The area occupied by the sensory membranes in a black bear's nose is a hundred times greater than that in a human's nose. Bears are believed to have a sense of smell rivaling that of a bloodhound. In the palate is a Jacobson's organ, or vomeronasal organ, a region of chemically sensitive nerve endings that greatly enhances the perception of airborne scent; to use this specialized structure, a bear lifts its snout, opens its mouth wide, and laps at the air while inhaling. As well as sniffing out food, a bear uses its sense of smell to steer clear of other bears and avoid unnecessary confrontations throughout much of the year, and to find a mate during the breeding season.

A bear's hearing is at least as good as a human's, and probably better. Some scientists believe that bears, like dogs, can hear sounds in the ultrasonic range, too high-pitched for humans to detect.

In watching bears stand on their hind legs and seemingly peer about, observers have concluded that the animals have poor eyesight. Black bears are believed to be nearsighted, which may be an adaptation helping them forage for small items close at hand. Yet bears can discern movement from a long way off, which is useful for finding prey and avoiding enemies. Experiments have shown that black bears can see in color, helping them discern and harvest foods such as berries.

A bear's eyes are directed forward in its skull, an arrangement that lets an animal see stereoscopically and judge distances with precision. In common with other creatures that depend to a certain extent on night vision, bears possess a tapetum lucidum, a layer of reflective cells at the back of the eyeball. When a light image passes through the retina, it is absorbed, stimulating vision cells; if very dim, the image may not be detectable on its first passage. The mirrorlike tapetum accentuates the image and bounces it back, flashing it to the receptor cells a second time. The tapetum causes the glow, or eye shine, seen when car headlights or a flashlight illuminate a bear at night.

Bears' paws are sensitive and dextrous. The five digits on each paw are tipped with prominent claws that cannot be retracted. Bears use their claws to protect themselves from foes and to pin down and grip prey, tear apart rotting logs to find insects, dig rodents and bulbs out of the ground, and scoop fish out of the water. A black bear's strongly curved claws dig into tree bark, letting it climb easily. A grizzly's straighter, longer claws are better suited to digging, and most grizzlies cannot ascend trees, unless the tree offers a series of well-placed limbs over which the bear can hook its paws. A polar bear's claws are thick and sharp-pointed, letting it snag and hold on to slippery seals, the bears' primary prey.

Bears have a high level of curiosity. When researchers gave various objects to captive black bears, the bears fixed more attention on the objects—turning them, sniffing them, chewing on them—than did other carnivores that were tested, including dogs, raccoons, and big cats. An active curiosity and a high level of intelligence allow bears to exploit a range of foods. Cubs follow their mother around and learn to eat different items by mimicking her. They also pick up and manipulate all sorts of objects, biting and gripping them with their teeth, a behavior that may help them discover new foods. Bears have a propensity to explore and locate new food sources, and their ability to learn helps them adapt to changes in the environment.

Because of their curved claws, black bears generally have an easier time getting into trees than grizzlies.

A physiologically based adaptation to a hostile environment—and an accompanying shortage of food—is hibernation. Except for the polar bear, northern bears feed heavily in summer and fall, building up body fat. Then they take shelter in a den (some bears "den" by simply lying on the ground) and fall into a deep sleep. A bear does not sink into the extreme torpor of a hibernating woodchuck or ground squirrel, but its body temperature drops and its heart rate slows. The body's metabolism keeps functioning by burning stored fat. Depending on where it lives, a bear may hibernate for up to six months a year, or half its life.

Bears face many perils. Mortality is highest in cubs, which may die in accidents, from malnutrition, and from predation by older bears, big cats, wolves, and other carnivores. Cubs and adults may be killed by fires, falls, rock and snow avalanches, collapsed dens, drowning in dens, starvation, getting struck by vehicles, and legitimate hunting and illegal poaching by humans; some bears end up being euthanized by game wardens because they repeatedly venture close to humans. Bears suffer from internal parasites, including hookworms, tapeworms, and roundworms. They can contract pneumonia, trichinosis, rabies, canine distemper, brucellosis, leptospirosis, and other diseases. They are host to many external parasites, including fleas and ticks.

Compared with other animals, bears have the potential to live for a long time. Wild black bears have survived past the age of thirty, and females in their late twenties have successfully raised litters. Grizzlies in captivity have lived beyond forty-five years, and wild grizzlies have been found to be as old as thirty-five. But most bears don't live that long. The average life span for a wild grizzly has been estimated at less than six years.

Evolution and Taxonomy

The fossil record suggests that 20 to 25 million years ago, in Europe, the first bear evolved from a group of bearlike dogs. Taxonomists call this proto-bear *Ursavus elmensis*; about the size of a fox terrier, it probably lived in forests, was a capable climber, and ate insects and small vertebrates. From this pint-size progenitor, around 5 million years ago arose the bears of genus *Ursus*, one of the three genera in which are placed the eight species of bears living today. All three species native to North America—black bear, grizzly bear, and polar bear—belong to genus *Ursus*. The black bear and the grizzly migrated here from Eurasia by crossing the Bering Straits land bridge during the ice ages.

The ice ages occurred during the Pleistocene epoch, from 1.5 million to about 10,000 years in the past, when fluctuating global temperatures caused northern glaciers to periodically extend southward and retreat northward. The Pleistocene has been called the Age of Mammals; a tremendous variety of mammalian species roamed the earth then, evolving—or going extinct—in response to factors such as climate change, competition with other species, and the rise of hunting humans. In North America alone lived all the mammals of today, plus elephants, camels, wild horses, asses, zebras, ground

During the Pleistocene epoch, the short-faced bear lived in North America. This great carnivore may have killed prey as large as mature bison, young mastodons and mammoths, and musk oxen. Some scientists think it preyed on the grizzly bear, keeping the latter species from populating the continent after it had migrated across the Bering Straits land bridge.

sloths, llamas, tapirs, and a host of predators including dire wolves, wild dogs, sabertooths, scimitar cats, jaguars, cheetahs, and American lions. The mammalian fauna of Eurasia was equally diverse and prolific.

A Pleistocene bear of Europe, now extinct, was the cave bear, *Ursus spelaeus*. This massive bruin grew as large as the biggest present-day Alaskan brown bears. Its fossilized remains have been found from Spain to Siberia, mainly in caves, where the bears probably hibernated. Some paleontologists have suggested that humans may have contributed to the demise of this great bear; others, noting that no signs have been found of butchering or tool marks on cave bear bones, believe humans did not have an impact on the *Ursus spelaeus* population. The huge, elongated molars of the cave bear were clearly adapted for crushing and grinding plants. The cave bear has been judged "the least carnivorous of carnivores, and the most bearish of bears," exemplifying the full expression of an evolutionary trend from a small-bodied carnivore (*Ursavis elmensis*) to a large-bodied omnivore. An extinct North American variant, the Florida cave bear (*Tremarctos floridanus*), seemingly evolved along a parallel path.

An especially fearsome Pleistocene predator was the short-faced bear, *Arctodus simus*. Larger than today's brown bears of Alaska, the short-faced bear was rangy and long-legged and stood over 6 feet tall at the shoulder— perhaps the biggest bear that ever prowled the earth. *Arctodus simus* was a dedicated meat eater. Its short, broad snout, similar to that of a lion or tiger, let it seize prey in a powerful killing grip, and it had large carnassial teeth for shearing off flesh. Fossils of the short-faced bear, sometimes called the bull-dog bear, have been found from Alaska to Pennsylvania and south to Central America. It seems likely that this monstrous carnivore killed prey as large as mature bison, young mastodons and mammoths, and other, smaller bears. Some scientists believe that the short-faced bear preyed on the grizzly bear, keeping it from spreading throughout North America after it had migrated across the Bering Straits into the northwestern part of the continent.

Bears Worldwide

Only three continents do not have bears: Africa, Australia, and Antarctica. Eight species of bears exist in the world today: American black bear, grizzly or brown bear, polar bear, spectacled bear, Asiatic black bear, sun bear, sloth bear, and giant panda bear. The first three species inhabit North America; they are treated at greater length in the next chapter and throughout the rest of the book. Following are descriptions of the five bear species found in other parts of the world, plus a description of the brown bear of Eurasia.

Spectacled Bear (*Tremarctos ornatus*)

The spectacled bear, also called the Andean bear, is the largest carnivore and the only bear inhabiting South America. It lives in the Andes Mountains in Venezuela, Colombia, Ecuador, Peru, Bolivia, and perhaps in isolated parts of

Brazil, Argentina, and Panama. The spectacled bear gets its name from whitish or yellowish markings around its eyes that look like spectacles or eyeglasses. The body fur is black and shaggy. Adults stand about 30 inches at the shoulder and weigh 175 to 275 pounds. Males are a third larger than females, and very large males can weigh up to 385 pounds.

Spectacled bears use a range of habitats, including lowland savannas, coastal desert scrub, foothills, moist forests, and alpine meadows. People have converted many of those lands to agriculture, and today spectacled bears are largely confined to steep, forested mountain slopes. Spectacled bears eat berries, palm leaves, palm nuts, orchid bulbs, and bromeliad hearts. Excellent climbers, they often ascend tall trees to get at figs and other tropical fruits. Insects and small animals make up an estimated 5 percent of the diet. Females give birth to cubs at the end of the winter rainy season, when food is plentiful. Scientists believe that two is the average litter size. Spectacled bears do not hibernate.

People kill spectacled bears for their meat and their fat, a traditional medicine for treating rheumatism. The bears are also shot when they damage cultivated fruits, sugarcane, and corn. The greatest threat to *Tremarctos ornatus* is the loss of its habitat to farming and logging. Biologists know little about the ecology and behavior of the spectacled bear, which lives in an unstable part of the world where conducting fieldwork can be very dangerous. No one knows how many spectacled bears survive today. The World Conservation Union (IUCN), an international organization of scientists and wildlife experts, lists the species as "vulnerable," or "facing a high risk of extinction in the wild in the medium-term future."

Asiatic Black Bear (*Ursus thibetanus*)

Also known as the Tibetan black bear, Himalayan black bear, and moon bear, this close relative of the American black bear lives in moist broad-leaved forests from northern Pakistan and Afghanistan eastward through the Himalayas to Vietnam and north into China. Separate populations occur in southeastern Russia, Korea, Japan, and Taiwan. A cream-colored, V-shaped marking resembling a crescent moon stands out on the bear's chest; the rest of the animal is black, save for a brown muzzle and white chin. The fur on the shoulders and neck forms a thick, prominent ruff. It's believed that the American black bear (*Ursus americanus*) and the Asiatic black bear belonged to the same species as recently as 3 to 4 million years ago and split off from each other during the ice ages.

Males weigh 250 to more than 400 pounds and are 5 to 6 feet long and slightly more than 3 feet tall when standing on all fours. Females are somewhat smaller. Asiatic black bears feed on plants, fruits, nuts, pine seeds, insects, and carrion. At times, they prey on deer, boars, other wildlife, and domesticated animals. Adept at climbing, Asiatic black bears sometimes rest in trees, in sloppy-looking nests made of twigs and branches. In northern areas, individuals hibernate in winter.

The smallest bear living on earth is the sun bear of southeast Asia; adults are 4 to 5 feet long and weigh between 60 and 145 pounds. Polar bears are the largest species, and the bigger males can weigh more than 1,500 pounds and stand 5 feet tall at the shoulders.

Asiatic black bears have a reputation for being short-tempered and aggressive; in Japan alone, each year black bears kill several people and injure ten to twenty. The bears are hunted heavily in Japan, including within the national parks. Across the species' range, people kill Asiatic black bears for food (in China, the paws are considered a particular delicacy) and for their body parts, especially their gallbladders, which are used in medicinal treatments. In Pakistan and India, mother bears are sometimes shot and their young captured and trained to walk upright, ride bicycles, and dance in roadside shows and circuses. The population of *Ursus thibetanus* has fallen drastically in recent decades as a result of poaching and the widespread destruction of forested habitats.

Sun Bear (*Ursus malayanus*)

The sun bear lives in dense tropical forests in Southeast Asia, from India east to Malaysia and Indonesia. The sun bear and South America's spectacled bear are the only bears that dwell south of the equator. About half the size of the American black bear, *Ursus malayanus* is the smallest of the eight living bear species. Adults are 4 to 5 feet long and weigh 60 to 145 pounds, with females 10 to 20 percent smaller than males. The short, black fur is interrupted by a yellowish white blaze on the chest, which earns this bear its name, although not all sun bears have this marking.

Accomplished climbers, sun bears often sleep in trees, in nests that they build out of broken branches. They eat earthworms, termites, wild bees and their larvae and honey (in some areas, the sun bear is known as the honey bear), birds, small reptiles and mammals, fruits, and other vegetation. Sometimes they damage crops, including oil palms. They are mainly nocturnal and do not hibernate. Females may give birth to cubs year-round.

Tropical deforestation and poaching have reduced the population of the sun bear, although to an unknown extent. The biologist Christopher Servheen, in his report *The Status and Conservation of the Bears of the World*, terms the sun bear "the least known of the bears in the world."

Sloth Bear (*Ursus ursinus*)

The sloth bear occurs in India, Nepal, Bhutan, Sri Lanka, and possibly Bangladesh. It is most widespread in the dry deciduous forests of India. The sloth bear's fur is long and shaggy, particularly across the shoulders; its belly fur is thin. The long fur may insulate against heat, and the sparsely furred belly may help the animal shed excess heat. Most sloth bears are black, although a few are cinnamon- or reddish-colored. A U-shaped patch of white marks the chest. Adults are 4 1/2 to 5 1/2 feet long and stand just under 3 feet tall at the shoulder. They weigh 150 to 300 pounds.

Sloth bears eat fruits, fleshy flowers, honey, carrion, and cultivated crops. But the main item in the bears' diet is insects, mostly termites and ants. The sloth bear lacks incisor teeth on its upper jaw and has a flexible snout and a high, hollowed-out palate. After it sniffs out a termite colony, the bear uses its

3-inch-long front claws to dig through the sun-baked earth into the insects' chambered nest. Then it forms its large, highly mobile lips into a tube and sucks adult insects and larvae into its mouth.

Females usually have litters of two or three cubs. The mother carries her young on her back, with the cubs clinging to her thick fur. By carrying her cubs, the mother may be better able to defend them against predators such as hyenas, leopards, and tigers. Sloth bears occasionally maul and kill people. Poachers kill adults and sell cubs to itinerant folk who train the young bears to "dance" in street shows; in India, an estimated 1,000 sloth bears are in captivity. Biologists estimate the population of *Ursus ursinus* at 7,000 to 10,000 worldwide. IUCN lists the sloth bear as a "vulnerable" species, threatened by the loss of its habitat to logging and clear-cutting of forested land for agriculture.

Giant Panda Bear (*Ailuropoda melanoleuca*)

Scientists studying the molecular genetics of bears believe that the giant panda branched off from the ursine family tree between 25 and 18 million years ago, making it the oldest of the eight living bear species. Fossils show that the giant panda was once widespread throughout China, but today it is restricted to six small forested areas on the edge of the Tibetan Plateau in central China.

Panda bears are colored black and white: the face is white, with the ears and areas around the eyes black; the forelegs are black, with a black band extending up and over the back; the neck and rump are white; and the hindlegs are black. Why such a boldly contrasting pattern? Biologist George Schaller, who has studied pandas in the wild, offers this explanation: "Pandas generally avoid contact [with each other], they are silent, their habitat is dense, and their vision is not acute. In such a situation a conspicuous coat may help prevent too close an encounter" from taking place—an encounter that could lead to an injury-causing fight.

Short and squat, pandas can move easily through thick vegetation. Adults are 5¹/2 to slightly over 6 feet long. Mature males weigh 190 to 275 pounds, about the weight of an average American black bear; females are 10 to 20 percent lighter. More than 99 percent of a panda's diet consists of the leaves, stems, and shoots of bamboo. Evolution has equipped the panda to process large volumes of this low-energy plant food. Each front paw has an elongated wrist, covered with a pad of skin, that operates like an opposable thumb, letting the animal grasp and manipulate bamboo stems. Large molars, a massive skull (a panda's head is exceptionally large in relation to its body, compared with other bears), and heavy jaws work in concert to pulverize the bamboo. The tough lining of the esophagus wards off splinters, and a muscular stomach keeps the bamboo churning to speed up digestion. To maintain its weight, an adult panda may feed for fifteen hours daily, consuming 22 to 40 pounds of leaves and stems.

Giant pandas live in cool, damp mountain forests at altitudes of 4,000 to more than 11,000 feet. Pandas have thick, woolly fur to insulate their bodies.

Because they rely on low-energy food, pandas do not build up enough body fat to let them hibernate, so they must remain active year-round. Pandas have a low reproductive rate. Females do not mature sexually until they are at least four years of age. A female may have up to three cubs in a litter, but she is rarely able to raise more than one of them successfully. Cubs usually leave their mothers when a year and a half old. Under optimum conditions, a female will produce approximately one cub every two years.

Between 700 and 1,000 giant pandas survive in the wild. IUCN classes the species as "endangered," or "facing a very high risk of extinction" in the near future. The giant panda's existence is threatened by humans cutting down bamboo forests to make farmland, by poaching, and by periodic die-offs of extensive stands of bamboo, which is a natural part of the plant's growth cycle.

Eurasian Brown Bear (*Ursus arctos*)

Today scientists consider the brown bear of Europe and Asia to be the same species as the grizzly bear of North America. Although extirpated from much of its former range, *Ursus arctos* holds on in pockets in long-settled Europe, including Spain, southern France, Italy, Austria, the Balkan states, Poland, Czechoslovakia, Romania, Bulgaria, Norway, Sweden, and Finland. Some of the remnant populations have dangerously few members (100 or fewer); the populations are not linked to each other by travel corridors, so they cannot exchange genetic material, and inbreeding has become a problem. A fairly healthy population of brown bears—around 120,000—exists in the former Soviet Union. The nation with the next largest population of brown bears is Romania, with about 5,500 in the Carpathian Range. Brown bears also inhabit parts of Turkey, Iran, Pakistan, Afghanistan, India, China, North Korea, and the northernmost Japanese island, Hokkaido.

Across this vast range, *Ursus arctos* shows great variation in color, size, and behavior. Following centuries of persecution by humans, European brown bears have become extremely furtive and wary, seldom leaving wooded cover and foraging for food at dusk and at night. They are much less aggressive toward people than are grizzlies. European bears have evolved to become smaller and darker than other brown bears, which probably helps them hide in their forested habitats. In the wilds of northern Russia, brown bears look and behave more like the grizzlies of North America.

Biologists have begun to monitor European bears, and efforts to restore and augment populations have begun in Italy, Austria, and Scandinavia. Bears from Slovenia have been trapped and released in the Pyrenees Mountains in Spain. The growing Slovenian population is believed to be expanding naturally into Austria.

2

North American Species

American Black Bear (*Ursus americanus*)

The range of the American black bear stretches from Newfoundland to Florida in the east and from Alaska to Mexico in the west. It takes in all or part of thirty-eight states, much of northern Mexico, and every Canadian province except Prince Edward Island. Black bears live in a variety of wooded and partially wooded settings, including mountains, lowlands, swamps, deserts, and the fringes of the arctic tundra. Biologists estimate the population of *Ursus americanus* at 400,000 to 750,000 continentwide, with the greatest concentrations in the forests of the Northeast, the Upper Midwest, and the Pacific Northwest.

Most black bears are black in color. Some individuals have a white V or blaze on the chest, and many have brown or tan muzzles. The nose is black, and the eyes are dark brown to almost black. Because the first bears encountered by settlers in North America were black, the species was given the name black bear. But not all black bears are black: coat color in bears is influenced by as many as ten separate genes, yielding many possible shades and color patterns, and perhaps the greatest color variation of any carnivore species.

The black color phase predominates in the East, Midwest, Pacific Northwest, Canada, and Alaska, with the occasional brown or cinnamon-colored individual showing up in those areas. In the drier regions of the West, an increasing percentage of black bears are a tawny or cinnamon color; one study in Colorado found that more than 80 percent of black bears were brown. The pale coat picks up less solar heat than a black pelt, which may prevent an ani-

The black bear, Ursus americanus

A cinnamon-colored black bear on a kill. The cinnamon phase is common in dry habitats such as the open woodlands of the American West.

mal from overheating in the more open western woodlands. Some scientists suggest an alternate reason for the pale coloration: it mimics the grizzly bear's fur, a pattern that may have evolved to bluff away potential predators.

In three areas of British Columbia resides the Kermode bear (named after Canadian zoologist Francis Kermode), which comes in a spectrum of colors: black, creamy, chestnut, yellow, bluish gray, and orangish. Southeastern Alaska is home to the glacier bear, whose bluish white coat blends in with its icy home. In the past, these different color phases were classified as separate species, but today they are considered subspecies, or races, of *Ursus americanus*.

The muzzle of the black bear is relatively narrow and straight compared with the broader, slightly upturned snout of the grizzly bear. The ears are rounded, and they are larger than a grizzly's ears. Biologists believe that the black bear has prominent ears so that individuals can send social signals to one another in the wooded, low-light settings where *Ursus americanus* lives.

Black bears vary greatly in size. A mature female in an area where food is scarce may weigh less than 100 pounds. In autumn, having laid on fat before

These silhouettes show the body profiles and relative sizes of the three North American species: black bear (top), grizzly bear (middle), and polar bear (bottom).

winter, a large, older male in a rich habitat can top 800 pounds—heavier than grizzly bears in many locales. In August 2001, a fifteen-year-old boar was killed by a car in Manitoba; he weighed 856 pounds, and biologists speculated that the bruin might have weighed 900 or even 1,000 pounds by the time he went into hibernation in November. But it's unusual for a male black bear to weigh in excess of 600 pounds. The following are average sizes and weights: 2 to 3 feet tall at the shoulders, when standing on all fours; 4^1/$_2$ to 6 feet long, including a 4- to 5-inch tail; and 150 to 400 pounds. In general, males are 33 to 50 percent larger than females.

Black bears are often characterized as adaptable, and of all the North American bear species, they have proven the most capable of living alongside humans and in habitats modified by human activities. Perhaps because there were so many huge, fierce predators around during the Pleistocene epoch—everything from lions to dire wolves to short-faced bears the size of ponies—black bears evolved to be somewhat timid, inclined to flee from any potential danger or shinny up a tree when threatened. Black bears, particularly young and lightweight ones, climb up trees in a series of quick, humping bounds; they almost run up the trunks. And since *Ursus americanus* inhabits forested settings, this avenue of escape almost always remains open.

Black bears live in a host of habitats: dense rain forests in the Pacific Northwest; the sparse montane woodlands of the Desert Southwest; cypress swamps in the Deep South; the fertile hardwood forests of the Mid-Atlantic states and New England; lodgepole pine woodlands in the Rockies; redwood forests in California and Oregon; and along the edge of the tree line in northern Canada and Alaska.

Black bears have even begun colonizing the treeless tundra, perhaps in places where grizzlies once occurred but have been extirpated by humans. One such area is northern Labrador and the Ungava Peninsula in northern Quebec east of Hudson Bay. There are historical records of grizzlies inhabiting the region (though not all scientists believe in the validity of the records), and in the 1970s, an anthropologist unearthed a grizzly skull while excavating an eighteenth-century Inuit site on the Labrador coast. What's certain is that in this wild area, black bears have established a population more than 200 miles out onto the "barren ground," as the treeless tundra is known. There they have become more predatory, feeding on caribou—perhaps like the grizzlies that may have ruled the area in the past.

Despite the black bear's great adaptability and recent expansion into certain areas, in the last three centuries the species' range and population have shrunk. In the South and Midwest, much land has been cleared for agriculture, and fewer bears exist in those regions than in the past. In Florida and Louisiana, black bears have become increasingly rare in the wake of urban sprawl and habitat fragmentation. States with no black bears include Illinois, Indiana, Iowa, Kansas, North Dakota, and South Dakota. Recently, black bears have begun spreading from Virginia into Kentucky and from Arkansas into Oklahoma. The Northeast has more bears today than it did a century ago.

Several factors have contributed to this increase: Many abandoned farms have grown back into forest, creating excellent bear habitat. State and national parks and forests now safeguard many wooded acres. In the past, people considered bears vermin or dangerous creatures and shot them on sight; today black bears are valued as game animals, and state wildlife biologists manage their populations to remain stable or increase.

No longer persecuted so consistently, black bears have become less shy, and many now venture around rural dwellings and even into towns and the fringes of cities, where they find new and nutritious foods such as garden crops, birdseed, and garbage—foods that can increase the bears' survival and reproduction rates. But rubbing shoulders with people also puts bears in jeopardy. Many are killed by automobiles, and "nuisance bears" are trapped and relocated to more remote settings, placed in zoos, or in some cases euthanized.

Grizzly Bear (*Ursus arctos*)

With a scientific name that means "northern bear," *Ursus arctos* is found across the Northern Hemisphere in the largest distribution of any bear on earth. In Europe and Asia *Ursus arctos* is known as the brown bear. Most Americans call it the grizzly, a colloquial name describing a pattern of fur coloration—brown with a grayish, or grizzled, tinge—occurring on many bears in the western United States and Canada. Genetic studies have shown that the grizzly bear (*Ursus arctos horribilis*) is actually the same creature as the so-called Alaskan brown bear or Kodiak bear (*Ursus arctos middendorffi*), as well as the brown bears of Europe and Asia. Any and all of those members of the various subspecies or races of *Ursus arctos* could interbreed and produce fertile young. Up to ten subspecies are recognized worldwide.

TOO MANY BROWN BEARS

In 1918, the federal Bureau of Biological Survey published a report by the noted mammalogist C. Hart Merriam, in which the author recognized no less than eighty-six kinds of grizzly and brown bears in North America. It's true that the brown bear, *Ursus arctos*, shows a tremendous range of coloration and size. Today, thanks to chromosome analyses and other modern scientific techniques, scientists have learned that there is but one species of brown bear worldwide. In most of North America, we call it the grizzly. In some parts of Alaska and western Canada, it goes by the name of brown bear.

Some authorities continue to separate *Ursus arctos* into two subspecies, or races, in North America, based on an appraisal made in the 1950s by biologist R. L. Rausch. According to Rausch, *Ursus arctos horribilis*, the grizzly, is found in the lower forty-eight states and in Canada and Alaska, including the coast of the Alaskan Peninsula. *Ursus arctos middendorffi*, the Kodiak bear, lives on Kodiak, Afognak, and Shuyak Islands off southern Alaska. Feeding on abundant salmon and berries, Kodiak bears can become huge, with some males approaching 1,500 pounds—almost as big as the largest polar bears.

The grizzly, or brown, bear, Ursus arctos

In this book, "grizzly" will be used to describe all of the brown bears of North America, and "brown bear" will refer to bears in Europe and Asia and to the species in general.

Paleontologists believe that the black bear (*Ursus americanus*) has inhabited North America for several million years, whereas the brown bear is a much more recent immigrant, having crossed the Bering land bridge from Asia to Alaska as recently as 30,000 years ago. In North America, grizzlies thrived in open, treeless habitats created by the retreating glaciers during the ice ages. *Ursus arctos* once ranged from northern Alaska and Canada south through California to Mexico, east to the Mississippi River, and possibly as far east as Labrador and the Ungava Peninsula in northern Quebec. Biologists estimate that from 100,000 to as many as 250,000 grizzlies inhabited the continent in 1800, with 50,000 to 100,000 of them south of Canada. Over the next two centuries, people eliminated many of the bears by shooting, trapping, and poisoning them, and by destroying or changing their habitat—turning it into farmland, housing developments, and highways. The great bears were gone from the Great Plains by 1900. California once had 10,000 grizzlies and was known as the Golden Bear State, but the species was extirpated there by the 1920s. Grizzlies had vanished from Oregon and the Southwest by the mid-1930s.

Today around 50,000 grizzlies remain in North America, most of them in the wilder parts of Canada and Alaska. In the lower forty-eight states, 900 to 1,200 grizzlies survive on less than 1 percent of the species' original range. The two largest populations live in the Greater Yellowstone Ecosystem, a 9,500-square-mile area centered on Yellowstone National Park in northwestern Wyoming, with 400 to 600 individuals, increasing by 2 to 4 percent yearly; and along the Continental Divide in northern Montana, including Glacier National Park, with 400 to 500 bears, thought to be stable or increasing. Other, smaller populations exist in the Cabinet-Yaak Ecosystem in northwestern Montana and northern Idaho, with 30 to 40 bears; the Selkirk Ecosystem in northern Idaho and northeastern Washington, with 40 to 50 bears; and the Northern Cascades Ecosystem in north-central Washington, with fewer than 20 bears.

The words bear and bruin derive from an old Germanic word meaning *brown*, and most grizzly bears are basically brown, but often their pelage shows additional tones of blond, auburn, silver, or black. From a distance, a grizzly's legs may look darker than the animal's sides and back. Like black bears, grizzlies molt during the summer, shedding their old fur and replacing it with a new pelt. When the new fur grows in, the outer guard hairs, which are longer than the insulating underfur, will be darker than the old, bleached-out hairs that they're replacing. So a freshly molted bear will wear a darker pelt than it did before its molt.

A grizzly bear's head is large. Its face has a "dished," or concave, appearance, with the muzzle ending in a broad, upturned snout. The grizzly possesses massive forelegs and a huge chest. A hump of muscle between the front shoulders provides power to the forelegs, for digging out food or excavating dens. (Black bears lack this muscular hump, although under some conditions,

Most grizzlies have brown fur, but the range of possible shades and tints is quite wide, as shown by this lighter-colored bear. Note the prominent hump of muscle between the shoulders.

and depending on how an individual happens to be standing, a black bear may appear to have a hump.) A grizzly's front claws—digging tools par excellence—are longer than its rear claws and may be 3 to 4$^1/2$ inches or more in length. The claws are usually pale in color. If a bear's claws are prominent enough that you can see them while the bear is walking, you are probably looking at a grizzly rather than a brown-phase black bear. The rear track of a big grizzly can be 14 inches long and 8 inches wide.

In coastal areas such as Kodiak Island in Alaska, where grizzlies feast on rich marine foods, mature males can weigh 1,000 to 1,500 pounds. These impressive creatures stand almost 5 feet tall at the shoulder when on all fours and approach 10 feet tall when standing on their hind legs. Among inland grizzlies, most adults weigh between 350 and 700 pounds. Individuals living north of the tree line on the arctic tundra are smaller, as are many brown bears of Europe.

Large and sturdy though they may be, grizzlies are also agile and quick. They can sprint over short distances to catch prey as large as elk. They can

A mature grizzly possesses a large skull. Its face has a "dished," or concave, appearance, with the muzzle ending in a broad, upturned snout.

dart this way and that to nab small, nimble creatures such as ground squirrels. Good swimmers, grizzly bears are able to catch salmon and other fish in the water; in the far north of their range, some of the bears hunt seals by swimming in the sea, much like polar bears. A grizzly's jaws are extremely powerful. When naturalist Terry Domico photographed a large male that researchers had caught in a leg snare, he watched the bruin vent its frustration on a 4-inch-diameter pine, snapping it off with a single bite. The bear had also chewed through several 6- and 8-inch-diameter trees nearby.

Grizzly bears, particularly females with cubs, are at least as famous for their ferocity as for their strength. The grizzly probably evolved from a forest-dwelling existence to a life on open, treeless terrain. Natural selection favored an animal with longer claws and a musculature that helped it dig for food. It also favored females that aggressively defended their young from other predators, since the bears had taken up residence in an environment offering no trees to climb. Today the grizzly is more apt than the black bear to attack other creatures, including people, particularly when it thinks they're a threat to its young. In his book *True Grizz*, the author and biologist Douglas Chadwick compares grizzlies to humans, both of which, he avers, "possess a lively intelligence and inquisitive nature along with the potential for monstrous behavior."

Polar Bear (*Ursus maritimus*)

Polar bears differ from other bears so markedly, in form, habits, and habitat, that it's hard to believe they are closely related to brown bears—so closely related, in fact, that polar bears and brown bears have mated in captivity and produced fertile offspring. Although the definition of a single species is a group of animals that can mate and produce fertile young, scientists nevertheless classify the polar bear as a species all its own. Paleontologists believe that *Ursus maritimus* branched off from *Ursus arctos* only 250,000 to 100,000 years ago, in the Pleistocene, perhaps in Siberia during a period of intense glaciation when the advancing ice cut off a northern population of brown bears, which then evolved separately. Should their divergent evolution continue, at some point polar bears will differ enough from brown bears that the two will not be able to produce offspring. In nature, brown bears and polar bears live in separate areas and have developed completely different reproductive behaviors and timing, so that the two types never mate.

The polar bear is considered to be the largest and most powerful land predator on earth. It is twice the size of a Siberian tiger and three times as large as an African lion. Adult males weigh 650 to more than 1,750 pounds. A large male can reach 5 feet tall at the shoulders while on all fours and 10 feet long from the nose to the tip of the tail; standing on its back legs, it towers 11 feet tall. Females are one-half to three-quarters the size of mature males and weigh an average of 330 to 700 pounds.

The pure white coat of the polar bear provides camouflage against ice and snow. The whiteness is interrupted by black eyes and a black nose and lips. As

The polar bear, Ursus maritimus

the arctic explorer Vilhjalmur Stefansson wrote, "No stone, no bare spot in the snow, no dark shadow is as black as the polar bear's nose." The fur is extremely dense. The long outer guard hairs are hollow, providing better insulating value. These hairs are clear, lacking in pigment altogether; they look white because they reflect and scatter visible light. Beneath that pale blanket, the skin is black, maximizing solar heat gain. In addition to its fur, a polar bear is insulated by a layer of fat, or blubber, up to 2 to 4 inches thick and lying just beneath the skin.

The hollow, air-filled fur, along with its blubber, help buoy a polar bear up in the water. The fur insulates when dry, but when the fur gets soaked, it is the blubber that provides a warm barrier against the cold. The name *Ursus maritimus* means "sea bear," and polar bears are strong swimmers. They can dive as deep as 15 feet and stay submerged for more than two minutes. They have been spotted swimming many miles out to sea.

The polar bear is almost exclusively a meat eater. It has long, sharp canine teeth. The carnassials—the flesh-shearing teeth between the canines and molars—are pointed and sharp-edged, in contrast to the flattened ones of brown and black bears. The polar bear has a proportionally smaller head than other bears, which it extends through holes in the ice to catch seals. Its long neck increases the polar bear's reach and allows the animal to hold its head above water while swimming. The front paws are huge—up to a foot in diameter. With partial webbing between the toes, they serve as paddles when the bear swims.

Dense fur pads the soles of the feet, improving traction on ice. The exposed skin on the bottom of the feet, in areas that contact the ground directly, is resistant to frostbite. The skin is also studded with numerous pliable, microscopic bumps that keep the feet from slipping. The external ears are small to minimize heat loss. Polar bears are believed to have fairly sharp vision; studies suggest that they may be somewhat farsighted. Their eyes appear to be sensitive to low light levels, important to an animal that hunts during the arctic winter. There is no evidence that polar bears ever suffer from snow blindness, so perhaps some as-yet-unknown adaptation shields their retinas from damaging ultraviolet rays reflected from snow and ice.

Polar bears live on the ice that covers the polar sea to the north of Alaska, Canada, Greenland, Norway, and the former Soviet Union. They do not occur at the South Pole. Many of the white bears come onto land during summer, when the sea ice melts. On land, they generally do not eat much food; in an adaptation not dissimilar to the hibernation of bears in more southerly latitudes, they enter a period of inactivity that some scientists call "walking hibernation." Some bears enter caves in the permafrost where they can keep cool and escape from biting flies.

Biologists recognize six core populations around the fringes of the Polar Basin, each centered on a traditional seal-hunting and denning area. A separate group of bears lives farther south, on and adjacent to Hudson and James Bays in Canada. Canada has 15,000 polar bears, most of them in the Northwest Territories. An estimated 25,000 to 40,000 polar bears exist worldwide, twice what the population is thought to have been in the 1960s, when the five nations where *Ursus maritimus* lives began cooperating to limit hunting and safeguard critical habitats.

Polar bears are vulnerable to oil spilled by tankers and discharged from ships. The oil can cause a bear's fur to clump together, reducing its insulating properties. Bears groom themselves by licking their fur, and if they accidentally ingest oil, it can poison them. Scientists have found that oil has caused intestinal ulcers, lung collapse, anemia, and kidney failure in polar bears. The increase in offshore drilling for oil in the Arctic could have significant effects on the white bears and their prey. Climate change is another environmental threat. Today global warming—which most scientists agree is caused largely by humans' burning of fossil fuels—is spurring an earlier breakup of sea ice in the spring and thinner ice year-round. These changes have great potential for disrupting the annual cycle of polar bear life.

3

Feeding Behaviors

Like all animals, bears eat to fuel their day-to-day metabolic processes, build up surplus energy for withstanding times of food scarcity, and successfully reproduce. In big-bodied creatures like bears, nutritional requirements are writ large. If a bear doesn't get enough food—enough *good-quality* food—it may starve to death while hibernating in winter or after it leaves its den in spring. It may not grow large enough to compete with others of its kind in finding a home range or courting a mate. If a female, it may lose several years of reproductive potential—and bears, with the exception of black bears in some particularly well-fed populations, are slow reproducers compared with most other mammals.

Black and Grizzly Bears: Voracious Omnivores

The Canadian biologist Stephen Herrero has studied bears extensively and written about their evolution and behavior. In *Bear Attacks: Their Causes and Avoidance*, Herrero writes, "Black and grizzly bears are the end products of meat eaters that were redesigned over millions of years to eat vegetation." He adds: "Bears have taken the occasional herbivory practiced by Carnivores and turned it into their essence. I imagine that ancestral bears that were best able to ingest and process vegetation were the most successful in surviving periods when game [animals] were scarce or were hard to catch."

Today's bears eat mainly plants, with various forms of vegetation—roots, stems, leaves, flowers, fruits, nuts—constituting more than three-quarters of the diet of most blacks and grizzlies. (The polar bear is a different story altogether; its unique feeding habits are discussed separately later in this chapter.) Bears show their carnivorous tendencies by readily eating meat when they can find or catch it. The flesh of other animals, including carrion, is extremely attractive to bears because its food value is higher than that of most vegetation. Bears are not effective enough as predators, however, to survive on meat alone.

Usually there isn't much food of any sort around when bears crawl out of their dens in spring, which can be any time from February in the southern states to late May in the Rocky Mountains and the high latitudes of Canada and Alaska. It may take several weeks for a bear to change over from the energy-conserving metabolism of hibernation to a state of full activity. During this transition period, bears are sluggish and do not eat or drink very much. In some habitats, bears lose weight through June and sometimes into July before good quantities of nutritious plant foods become available.

In the East and Upper Midwest, one of the earliest spring foods appears in low, swampy areas: skunk cabbage. As this hardy plant pushes up from the muck, it generates its own heat to keep its flower, shielded by vegetative tissue, at a constant temperature of 70 degrees F, warm enough to melt its way through snow and ice. Black bears eat the new leaves and flowers of skunk cabbage, avoiding the plants' older leaves, stem, and roots, which contain the mouth-stinging compound calcium oxalate. In the West, both black and grizzly bears seek out the related yellow skunk cabbage.

Bears eat crowberries, cranberries, and bearberries that ripened the previous fall and remained clinging to the plants over winter. They graze on dried plants left over from the year before, but they much prefer the tender new growth, higher in protein and lower in indigestible cellulose. Important spring plant foods include the shoots of grasses, sedges, and clovers, and succulent early-blooming flowers such as dandelions. Bears make up for the low caloric content of many springtime foods by packing them away in quantity; a researcher in Alaska reported finding 5 quarts of horsetail shoots in the stomach of a black bear.

A winter-killed deer, elk, moose, or bison represents a huge quantity of protein, and bears compete for these vernal bonanzas with wolverines, coyotes, foxes, eagles, and other scavengers. Bears sniff out the winterkills. They watch and listen for ravens feeding on a carcass, then home in for a meal. After feeding on a dead animal, a bear may cover what remains by pawing grass, sod, leaves, and sticks onto the carcass. Covering or burying a carcass masks odors that might draw in other scavengers, and it slows down decomposition—although rotting flesh scarcely deters a bruin, which eats hearty, maggots and all. A bear may remain near a carcass—either a winter-killed one or an animal taken as prey—for as long as two to three weeks. Herrero notes that a 700-pound elk "could make the difference between whether or not a pregnant grizzly would have cubs the next season," adding, "No wonder such food sources are so aggressively defended." In some instances, people unknowingly hiking past carcasses have been badly mauled and even killed by grizzly bears.

Bears often consume massive amounts of grass and other plants in the spring.

The grizzly is "systematic and forward-looking" in the way that it feeds on and protects carrion, writes naturalist Paul Schullery in *The Bears of Yellowstone*. The black bear, notes Schullery, "may drag meat to a more convenient spot to eat it, but blacks do not 'cache' meat, that is they do not formally hide it by concealment or burial to save it for later."

The black bear's curved, 1- to 1 1/2-inch-long claws and the structure of its back and shoulder muscles aid it in climbing trees, as opposed to digging roots and rodents out of the ground, which is a specialty of the grizzly. In spring, black bears scale trees to get at the emerging leaves and catkins, the small reproductive structures of aspens, willows, and related species. Black bears climb into slender aspens; when the trees start to bend, the bruins hang on by their teeth and let their weight break the saplings down. Bears strip leaves from branches by drawing the twigs through the gap, known as a diastema, between their canine and molar teeth.

On the slopes of the Rocky Mountains, grizzlies follow the line of the retreating snowpack, where new greenery continues to emerge for weeks on

The long claws of grizzlies are an adaptation for digging out roots and bulbs. Claws are also used for snagging and subduing prey animals and in fights with other bears.

end. They use their long, straight claws to dig up glacier lilies, spring beauties, peavine, wild onion, and other plants; the bears feed on the roots and bulbs, in which are concentrated nutrients to fuel the plants' impending growth. Plants in genus *Hedysarum*, also called bear root, are a favorite spring food. Grizzlies, with their heavy jaws and teeth, eat many more roots, bulbs, corms (fleshy underground stems resembling bulbs), and tubers than do black bears. Blacks tend to rely more on green vegetation and, later in the year, on berries, neither of which require massive jaws and dentition to process.

Both grizzlies and, more frequently, black bears bite the outer bark of trees, peel it away, and use their front teeth to scrape up the underlying sapwood, which is soft and sweet. This feeding method leaves long strips of bark hanging loose, and sometimes it girdles the tree, killing it. Bears relish the inner bark of many trees, both hardwoods and softwoods. In the Pacific Northwest, blacks damage so many conifers in commercial forests that some companies hire professional hunters to shoot the bears. Other forestry firms put out pelleted feed to divert the bark chewers.

Insects are an important source of fat and protein. Bears eat a wide variety of insects, including some so small it hardly seems worth their while to feed on them—ants, for instance. A bear will wallop an anthill, then place its paw on the heap's swarming center. When enough of the hill's frantic residents have crawled onto the paw, the bear licks them off. (Some biologists believe the acidic taste of ants is especially attractive to bruins.) Bears eat beetles, crickets, grasshoppers, and caterpillars—even tent caterpillars, despite their irritant protective hairs. Bears dismantle rotten logs, then use their long, sticky tongues to lap up any beetles or ants or grubs that have been exposed. They eat wasps and bees and the honey stores and larvae of these communal insects, wiping the stinging workers off their muzzles as they feed. In the mountains of the West, grizzlies dine on cutworm moths that shelter by day beneath rock rubble. The moths spend the summer gleaning sugars from alpine flowers; by autumn they are almost 75 percent fat and represent one of the richest sources of energy a bear can find. In springtime, bears also check out snowbanks for insects that hatched from nearby streams, landed by accident on the snow, and became numbed by the cold.

Bears sniff out and appropriate the caches of nuts stored below ground by rodents—and, if given a chance, scarf up the rodents as well. In the Rockies, grizzlies dig out marmots, ground squirrels, mice, and voles. To get at the rodents, the bears dig up and turn over immense volumes of ground. Grizzlies sometimes dig so deep that they disappear from view. Acre upon acre can end up covered by holes and mounds. Recent studies in Glacier Park show that grizzlies feeding on roots and rodents rake and plow up more land than any other wildlife species. In the process, they bring nitrogen from lower levels in the soil up to the surface. They also spread around plants' seeds, which sprout in the newly enriched earth. Notes Douglas Chadwick in *True Grizz*, "This fertilizing effect causes vegetation such as glacier lilies and spring beauties to grow more vigorously and produce more seeds than they do in undisturbed sites."

A particularly attractive spring food is garbage: tasty, loaded with calories, and highly digestible. Because garbage-eating bears may lose their fear of humans, many state wildlife agencies prohibit feeding bears and allowing them access to garbage. Parks and campgrounds may use bear-proof trash bins to discourage foraging bears.

Bears dine on snails, centipedes, crayfish, crabs, shellfish, frogs and other amphibians, snapping turtles, birds, birds' eggs, and nestlings. In June 1986, an ornithologist studying waterfowl nesting colonies in Canada's Northwest Territories documented five grizzlies destroying some 2,500 brant nests and more than 3,000 snow goose nests, and eating approximately 24,000 eggs. (The ornithologist reported that the bears came down with a terrific case of diarrhea.) Bears have been spotted killing and eating eagle nestlings when the parent birds nested on or too close to the ground.

Some bears eat dirt—perhaps for protein-rich earthworms or for trace elements. Others chow down on creosote-painted wooden signs. They eat mushrooms. They consume rabbits, woodchucks, and any other small creatures they can nab. In the Deep South, black bears chew the hearts out of cabbage palms in April; come June, they rifle alligator nests for the reptiles' eggs. Female alligators usually guard their clutches fiercely. One particularly determined scientist wanted to see whether alligators defend their nests against marauding black bears, so he dressed up in a bear suit and went walking on all fours through Okefenokee Swamp. The alligators fled.

In the spring, bears keep an eye peeled for large prey, including winter-weakened animals. A grizzly will chase a herd of grazers at an easy lope, looking for an animal that can't quite keep up. The bear will run in close to a flagging elk, rear up on its hind legs, grasp the elk over the rump, and throw all of its weight onto the animal. The elk's hindquarters collapse; the bear uses its jaws to seize the hapless creature by the neck, killing the animal by shaking it until its spine snaps or biting down and asphyxiating it. A bear may run along next to an elk, slapping it in the head repeatedly until the creature falls down in a daze. Grizzlies have been seen killing fully grown elk, moose, bison, and musk oxen, although not often do they tackle such dangerous prey. On the island of Newfoundland, black bears sometimes prey on adult caribou. During an elk census in Yellowstone National Park in May, a biologist in a helicopter watched a black bear drive a mature bull elk into deep snow, where the bruin was able to kill it.

Young subadult grizzlies—littermates that have remained together after parting from their mother—may team up to bring down large animals. The most persistent and successful hunters of large prey are, in fact, young adult grizzlies—not because they are faster or more agile than older bears, but because the dominant bruins have learned to wait until a kill is made and then chase the youngsters off the carcass. With its formidable size and strength, a bear may steal prey from a pack of wolves, a puma, a bobcat, or some other lesser predator. In Alaska, biologists observed that wolves usually abandoned carcasses to grizzlies but were less likely to give them up to blacks. Bears even eat bears: grizzlies sometimes prey on blacks, and large black bears occasionally catch and kill smaller members of their own species.

Both black and grizzly bears eat the young of other mammals, particularly those of the family Cervidae, which includes deer, elk, moose, and caribou. Black bears are major predators of white-tailed and mule deer fawns, locating their quarry by sight or smell. If very young, a fawn may freeze in place—with predictable results. An older fawn will try to escape by fleeing, but bears run down and catch many. A bear kills a fawn by slamming it down with a paw, then suffocating it with a sustained bite to the neck. Or the bruin delivers a killing bite: puncture wounds made in skulls by bear canine teeth can be $1/2$ inch in diameter. Bears are not humane killers, and sometimes a hungry bruin will begin feeding on a fawn before the creature has died. A bruin may tear apart and consume an entire fawn, including skin, skull, and bones, at a single sitting. One biologist watched a large black bear kill a fawn and eat all but one foot in less than an hour.

In the 1970s, when researchers first began attaching radio collars to newborn cervids to learn their survival rates, the scientists were astonished at how many were killed by bears. A study in Utah showed that black bears killed almost 10 percent of mule deer fawns in a given area. Grizzlies killed 43 percent of moose calves in one Alaska study area, and black bears took 34 percent in another. An Idaho investigation determined that black bears killed 47 percent of elk calves in one local population. Some researchers suggest that bears seek out calving areas to prey on the vulnerable young of grazing animals. Others believe that bears and pregnant grazers simply come together in places that have abundant fresh, green plants.

Steven and Marilynn French spent many summers in the rolling uplands of Yellowstone National Park observing grizzlies hunting for elk calves. They report that a bear will move about through a sagebrush-covered area for several hours, periodically stopping to look around and sample the breeze. Like white-tailed and mule deer fawns, elk calves give off only a faint odor, and their coats are brown with white spots, a pattern that helps them blend in with the dappled light that penetrates the partly shaded areas where their

A grizzly bear and gray wolf moving in on an elk kill. In most cases, wolves will let grizzlies take a kill.

Grizzlies prey on the young of elk, moose, and deer, as do black bears.

mothers often temporarily leave them. The Frenches learned that bears some-times passed within 6 feet of a bedded calf without finding it. Using night-vision goggles, the researchers found out that bears hunt elk calves in the darkness as well as by day.

Within a week or two, elk calves and other young cervids (members of family Cervidae) become more mobile and start following their mothers about and feeding with them. At this point, the bears change their tactics: they hide behind vegetation, stalk as close as they can get, charge out of the brush, and try to run the young down. If, when chased, an elk calf makes a quick turn, it will usually escape, since a bear at full sprint cannot turn as nimbly. Doe deer and caribou cows usually do not defend their young, but cow elk and moose can be more protective. Sometimes a cow runs between her calf and a pursu-ing bear, a ploy that may break the bear's concentration and slow it down enough for the calf to get away. Or the female runs ahead of her calf, showing it the best escape route. Occasionally a cow elk or moose uses her heavy, sharp front hooves to pummel an attacking bear. Sometimes this desperate act suc-ceeds in driving the bruin off. When they are six to eight weeks old, young cervids usually have the strength and stamina to escape from a bear on their own. Most bears chase calves and fawns for about 100 yards before giving up.

In the past, some grizzly bears developed into prolific killers of domesti-cated cows, sheep, and horses. Nowadays, in a typical year, the approximately

1,000 grizzlies in the lower forty-eight states kill fewer than fifty cattle. During pioneer times, black bears also killed some livestock; one New Hampshire bruin was reported to have killed twenty-seven cows over a two-year period. Such transgressions usually brought down the wrath of settlers, who conducted mass hunts that often wiped out the stock-killing bruin along with other potentially aggressive bears to which it may have been genetically related.

As summer arrives, bears congregate on tributaries draining into large lakes and into the ocean, for it is up those freshwater streams and creeks that trout and salmon swim, returning to the areas where they hatched, there to spawn. Black bears fish in inland waters and coastal rivers from Washington to Alaska. From British Columbia to Alaska (and on the opposite side of the Pacific, on Russia's Kamchatka Peninsula), grizzlies feed heavily on salmon. Five species of salmon breed in tributaries that drain from North America into the Pacific, and local areas may see a succession of salmon runs during summer and fall. Salmon represent a rich, dependable food source; they are probably the main reason why the majority of grizzlies living on the planet today dwell within 100 miles of the Pacific.

Normally solitary, the bears come together by the dozens in prime fishing areas, such as zones below waterfalls and along shallow stretches of rapids, where the upstream progress of the salmon is slowed and large numbers of fish rest in pools and eddies. One fishing spot in particular—the McNeil River Falls Game Sanctuary in Alaska—has become a famous tourist attraction, where people pay for the privilege of watching grizzlies fish. The bears pay little or no attention to the human onlookers, so intent are they on catching and gorging on their prey.

Outdoor artwork often depicts bears slapping salmon out of the water, but a more usual method is for a bear to pin a fish against the stream bottom using one or both forepaws, then lower its mouth to secure the prize. Bears use many other techniques as well. They swim with their faces in the water, looking down, ready to seize salmon finning beneath. They chase the fish into shallows, where they can be nabbed more easily. Some bears catch jumping salmon in their jaws. Older, dominant bears claim and defend the best fishing locations, such as flat rocks below waterfalls. Younger bears may have to settle for fish that have been partially eaten and then discarded by other bears.

An adult grizzly may catch ten salmon in an hour and fifty during one day—far more than the creature can put in its stomach. At first a hungry bear will devour entirely any salmon it catches. Later it will ignore the protein-rich muscle tissue and instead concentrate on eggs, skin, and brains, which have a higher fat content. Gorging on fish fat lets a bear build up its own fat reserves rapidly. The body weight of salmon-fed bears can be 50 percent fat by autumn. Fish that bears kill but do not consume get eaten by foxes, ravens, eagles, and other scavengers.

After bears mate in early summer, they get down to the serious business of eating—to grow and maintain muscle mass, to layer on fat that will see them through the coming winter and spring, and in the case of females who have become pregnant, to prime their bodies for the development of fetuses and the eventual birth of cubs.

Biologists often refer to two general categories of autumnal vegetable foods as soft and hard mast. (*Mast* is an Old English word meaning the nuts of forest trees accumulated on the ground.) Both hard and soft mast are extremely important to bears, which may leave their home territories and travel as far as 100 miles to gain access to large quantities of those foods. Cubs probably remember prolific food sources that they visit with their mothers and return to them in future years after they're on their own.

Soft mast includes berries and other fruits rich in proteins and easily metabolized carbohydrates. On various parts of the continent, bears eat immense quantities of strawberries, juneberries, raspberries, blueberries, elderberries, salmonberries, soapberries, pin cherries, black cherries, wild grapes, cranberries, pokeberries, whortleberries, dewberries, and the fruits of apple, black-gum, sassafras, dogwood, and many other trees and shrubs. A bear will move its mouth along a fruit-laden branch, its lips and incisor teeth rapidly plucking off berries. It may lie sprawled on its belly in a patch of shrubs, using its paws to pull branches toward its mouth—no matter that dozens of stems are broken in the process. A bear doesn't pick every last berry off a bush, as a human forager might; instead, it shifts from one well-laden shrub to another, to maximize the volume of fruit it can stow away. A grizzly may devour thousands of berries a day when the shrubs and bushes are loaded. In the Yukon, by counting soapberry seeds in typical bear scats and estimating the number of scats a grizzly produced daily, one researcher concluded that a bear might eat as many as 200,000 berries per day.

A bear gulps down berries without chewing them. Its stomach mashes the fruit together; the pulp is digested, and the seeds or pits are expelled in the bear's feces. Bears generally do not crush seeds with their teeth. The seeds of many plants contain bad-tasting toxins to dissuade mammals from destroying them; after all, the "reason" a plant produces berries is to attract animals to eat its fruit and later to disperse intact, germinable seeds throughout the environment. The seeds of many plants are more apt to germinate after traveling through a bear's digestive tract: when the seeds are abraded against each other and bathed in acidic fluid, their coatings become more permeable to water and gases. Studies have shown that cow parsnip seeds have a 16 percent improved germination rate after having passed through a grizzly. Raspberry, chokecherry, and dogwood seeds are, respectively, two, three, and seven times more likely to sprout after black bears have processed them.

When Robert Inman and Michael Pelton of the University of Tennessee studied summer and fall feeding habits of black bears in the Smoky Mountains, they found that in terms of calories, soft mast made up one-quarter of the bears' diet, while hard mast—acorns, hickory nuts, beechnuts, hazelnuts— accounted for three-quarters. Nuts contain up to twice as much fat as does soft mast. Inman and Pelton judged oaks to be "the single most important food genus affecting black bear ecology in the southern Appalachians." Bears eat the

In northwestern North America, salmon swim up rivers to spawn in the areas where they hatched. Grizzlies feed heavily on the fish, sometimes catching the jumping salmon in their jaws. Gorging on fish fat lets a bear build up its own fat reserves rapidly.

acorns of red, white, and chestnut oaks, as well as many other oak (*Quercus*) species. There's even a shrubby oak, scarcely taller than a standing bear, known as bear oak—named after the bruins that relish its small, bitter nuts.

By climbing into oaks to feed, bears get first crack at the acorns before other ground feeders such as deer and wild turkeys can compete for the mast. And acorns eaten in the trees yield their maximum nutritional value: after falling to the ground, many become parasitized with the larvae of nut weevils and are further degraded by fungi and bacteria.

Inman and Pelton were surprised to discover the importance of one bear food most people have never even heard of: squawroot. This squat, spiky, tan-and-cream-colored plant lacks leaves and chlorophyll; it gets its nutrients by parasitizing the roots of trees, especially oaks. Squawroot grows in eastern North America from Nova Scotia southward. In their Tennessee study area, Inman and Pelton found that squawroot provided fully 15 percent of bears' calories. Bears seek out squawroot in late spring and early summer, before most fruits ripen. The researchers theorized that hard mast raises bears' reproductive rates, whereas high-energy spring and summer foods such as squawroot boost the survival of cubs already on the ground. Inman and Pelton suggest that an increasing bear population in Great Smoky Mountains National Park, as well as other parts of the Appalachians, may be caused in part by squawroot becoming more abundant in the region's maturing oak forests.

Beechnuts are a key food in the northern hardwood forest—the beech-birch-maple woodland stretching across many northeastern and upper midwestern states—where acorn-producing oaks are few. Black bears eat beechnuts that have fallen to the ground, carefully pushing aside the leaves with their paws and sniffing out the small, triangular nuts. They also climb to harvest beechnuts. Bears' sharp claws leave prominent black scars on the trees' smooth, pale gray bark. Sometimes a bear will sit in a beech crown for hours, wrestling nut-bearing boughs in toward its perch and often breaking them. Dead leaves remain clinging to bear-damaged branches for weeks after the bruin has moved on and the tree's other leaves have fallen; the conspicuous clusters of brown foliage and splintered limbs are known as "bear nests." Some bears actually use the structures as nests. Pennsylvania biologist Gary Alt found a nest, about 6 feet in diameter and almost 50 feet up in a beech, built out of twenty-seven broken limbs; it was sturdy enough that a bear slept in it for the first half of one winter.

Nut-bearing trees are more plentiful in the East than in the West. But western bears eat nuts, too. At high elevations in the Rockies grows whitebark pine, whose large, oily nuts are a favorite of bears. Blacks clamber into the trees' crowns and feed when the cones are still hanging; nonclimbing grizzlies wait for cones to fall, and they raid cones that red squirrels store in piles called middens on the ground and at the bases of trees.

In autumn, subtle changes in a bear's physiology heighten the animal's ability to digest fat, leading to a rapid weight gain. Bears develop tremendous appetites and enter a period termed hyperphagia, or feeding frenzy. They may feed for twenty hours at a clip. Grizzlies take in 20,000 to 30,000 calories and put on 2 to 3 pounds every twenty-four hours (25,000 calories is equivalent to fifty-eight fast-food quarter-pound hamburgers). An individual grizzly can down one-third of its body weight daily in fruit and 15 percent in meat; the fruit passes through the digestive system more rapidly than the meat. Bears eat any remaining berries and green vegetation; roots and tubers; crops, particularly corn; autumn-ripening fruit such as apples and pears; bees and hornets and their larvae and honey; carrion, including road-killed animals and game shot and unrecovered by hunters; and live prey, from chipmunks to caribou. A female grizzly under observation in Alaska's Brooks Range dug out and ate 357 ground squirrels during one autumn; the squirrels provided an average of 22,000 calories per day. (The bear ate other foods as well.) A male grizzly on Kodiak Island gained more than 200 pounds in seventy days. In the acorn-rich forests of Pennsylvania, a mature black bear weighed 348 pounds in midsummer; when recaptured two months later, he was 476 pounds.

Should soft or hard mast crops fail, blacks and grizzlies travel more widely in search of food, which often leads them into suburbs and near rural dwellings. Bears crawl into trash receptacles and wrestle the lids off garbage cans. They rummage in compost piles. They knock over beehives. They vacuum up birdseed and dog kibble, and break into coops for rabbits, chickens, and goats, and into cars for picnic lunches. Wildlife agencies field many more bear-damage complaints in years when natural foods are scarce.

When a bear has laid on enough fat to sustain it through winter—or, if it is a pregnant female, enough to get it through the lean season *plus* produce cubs—its appetite usually wanes. Although surrounded by rich foods, a bruin may simply stop feeding. If it is not yet time for denning, a bear may loaf for a few weeks before entering its den and lapsing into hibernation. Some bears—most notably grizzlies in comparatively mild climates, as on the islands off the coast of Alaska—may postpone hibernating or may not do so at all if food remains available through winter. In late autumn, all northern bears—except polar bears—are at their heaviest weights for the year.

Polar Bears: Dedicated Carnivores

The polar bear shares its harsh, demanding environment with a host of marine mammals, from 150-pound ringed seals to walruses weighing more than a ton, as well as several species of whales. All of those creatures must breathe in oxygen from the air, and it is at the edge of the sea ice, or at breathing holes in the ice, that the white bear encounters its prey.

The ringed seal, the most abundant and widely distributed marine mammal in the Arctic, is the primary prey of *Ursus maritimus*. (The seals are themselves predators, eating fish and small, shrimplike invertebrates.) Ringed seals use their clawed flippers to scratch through the ice from below, forming breathing holes that they maintain even when the ice becomes as thick as 6 feet. During the long polar winter, a seal keeps three or four breathing holes open, periodically surfacing at these critical locations to take in air, and defending them against intrusions by other seals. Where snow and ice accumulate above a hole, a seal may hollow out a cave in which to rest or, if a female, to give birth to young.

Polar bears hunt seals using two main methods: waiting and stalking. When waiting for a seal, a bear lies on its belly on the ice next to a breathing hole. Ian Stirling, a Canadian scientist and the world's leading polar bear researcher, has watched bears wait at a hole for more than two hours, with an average time of fifty-five minutes per session. The bear lies motionless, relying on its body fat and thick fur to stay warm. As well as being comfortable for the bear, a supine position presents the smallest silhouette to a surfacing seal. (A persistent folk belief has the polar bear covering its highly visible black nose with a paw. In his many hours of observing, Stirling has never seen a bear do that.) When a seal surfaces, the bear lunges forward, grabs the creature in its jaws, and yanks it up through the breathing hole—even if the hole is smaller than the seal, in which case the seal is turned into an elongated, bloody pulp. The bear then bites the seal several times in the neck and head, killing it.

Bears stalk seals less frequently than they ambush them. When stalking, a bear sneaks toward a seal that has hauled itself out onto the ice, or one that the bear has smelled resting in its den. Using ice ridges and snowdrifts to conceal its movements, the bear creeps close. At the end of a stalk, it makes a short charge and seizes its prey, or it leaps onto the roof of a den, slamming down its forepaws to break through the crust, and grabs the seal within. A polar bear's sense of smell is so acute that often the bruin crashes into a den directly above its occupant. During the seals' breeding season—in April and May, just after the females have whelped their young—the rutting males have a rank, unpleasant odor, which taints their blubber and meat. One researcher found that bears rarely broke into the lairs of male seals, preferring to prey on the less odoriferous females and pups.

In winter, polar bears often hunt near polynyas, areas of ocean that remain ice-free as a result of winds, currents, tides, or upwellings of warm water. Polynyas cover an estimated 3 to 4 percent of the Arctic's surface area. These biological hot spots support a prolific growth of algae and plankton, which sustain large quantities of invertebrates; fish feeding on the invertebrates in turn attract seabirds, seals, and walruses. Whales also frequent polynyas.

Polar bears sometimes prey on walruses. Mainly they take calves and subadults, but large male polar bears can kill adult male walruses, which are

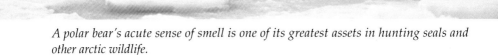

A polar bear's acute sense of smell is one of its greatest assets in hunting seals and other arctic wildlife.

more than 10 feet long, weigh up to 2,600 pounds, and defend themselves with their long, pointed tusks. When polynyas shrink during extended cold spells, walruses and whales may find themselves stranded in dwindling pools of open water—the only places where they have access to air. In northern Alaska, polar bears killed forty beluga whales trapped in open water surrounded by pack ice; subsequently, some thirty bears scavenged on the carcasses. In northern Russia, an observer saw a polar bear kill a beluga whale; when the whale surfaced at an opening in the ice, the bear used a forepaw to deliver a mortal blow to its head. In the Canadian Arctic, a marine biologist watched as a large bear waited on an ice floe; when a beluga calf swam past, the bear jumped on top of it and killed it with a bite to the head. At birth, beluga whales are 4 feet long and weigh 100 pounds. Adults are 1,000 to 3,000 pounds, and many carry scars on their bodies left by bear claws.

On rare occasions, polar bears kill musk oxen, especially when those animals travel across the sea ice when shifting from one habitat to another. Confronted by a predator, musk oxen will gather in a circle, with the young animals inside the ring and the adults, with their sharp horns, standing shoulder-to-shoulder, facing outward. Rather than attack a group of musk oxen, polar bears are more likely to tackle lone bulls separated from the defense of the herd.

In summer, the polar ice recedes and breaks up along its edges, and large channels called leads open in the ice. The sun melts the snow caves of seals. The seals molt in summer, shedding and replacing their winter fur, a process that makes them temporarily more susceptible to the water's chill. To keep warm, the seals frequently haul themselves out of the water and onto the ice. When basking, they remain vigilant, raising their heads approximately every twenty seconds, looking around and sniffing the air.

Bears spot or scent the seals from a distance and stalk or swim toward them. A bear may approach through open water, or it may swim beneath the ice, surfacing at a series of holes to take in air. Writes Stirling, "The bears have such control that they can surface, breathe, raise their heads slightly to look, and submerge without making a ripple in the water." Coming up next to a seal, the bear tries to grab the slippery prey before it can dive back into the water. In addition to ringed seals, polar bears catch and kill bearded seals weighing up to 770 pounds. Studies show that a polar bear is four times less likely to catch a seal in the open than one lying in its winter den. To fill its belly, a polar bear must spend more time hunting in the summer: nine to thirteen hours per day, compared with four to six hours in winter.

In summer, young seals are sheathed in fat, known as blubber, laid down after months of nursing on their mothers' milk. Blubber insulates seals and other arctic mammals, provides buoyancy to help them stay afloat in their watery realm, and stores calories against times when food is scarce. In essence, polar bears try to transfer blubber from the seals to their own bodies.

The period between April and July is a critical time for polar bears. They must maintain or increase their fat reserves to last them through summer, when hunting is less profitable—a reversal of the situation for grizzlies and black bears, which layer on fat during summer and autumn to sustain them during the lean months of winter. Some polar bears register tremendous weight gains: a seventeen-year-old female that weighed 218 pounds in November was 904 pounds when biologists recaptured her the following July. Researchers have estimated that simply to maintain its weight, an adult polar bear must eat 4 pounds of blubber or 11 pounds of muscle each day. In April and May, bears preferentially feed on the fat-rich skin and blubber of their kills and may ignore muscle tissue and viscera.

For a polar bear, blubber is a wonderfully efficient food: after the bear's digestive system has wrung the nutrients out of it, all that remains is carbon dioxide and water. The bear expels the carbon dioxide when it breathes and uses the water for its own internal needs. By contrast, when a bear eats muscle and viscera, the chief waste product is urea, which must be flushed out in the urine. Since urine is largely water, the bear must sacrifice precious fluids to rid itself of urea. To replenish those fluids, the bear is forced to eat snow; the snow must be melted inside the body, requiring the bear to burn precious calories to maintain its body temperature. Clearly, concentrating on eating blubber pays a polar bear big dividends.

Ursus maritimus can be an extremely efficient hunter. In his book *Bears*, Wayne Lynch writes of watching a young subadult female take four seals during a forty-two-hour span. Finally sated, she abandoned the last carcass after eating very little of it. Polar bears usually do not cache carcasses, but instead eat what they want and leave the rest behind. Individuals sometimes scavenge at kills left by other bears, and large, mature bears often steal kills away from smaller ones. Other animals, including ravens, gulls, and arctic foxes, feed on the partially eaten seal carcasses that a successful bear leaves in its wake. Land-based red foxes, wolverines, and wolves have all been spotted venturing onto the sea ice to feed on kills abandoned by bears. Polar bears are generally solitary, but when they find a bountiful source of food, such as a dead whale, they may gather by the dozens, with six or more individuals feeding side by side on the carcass at one time.

In summer, polar bears try to remain on the pack ice as long as possible so they can keep hunting seals. In some regions, such as the southern part of Hudson Bay, the ice melts completely, forcing the bears onto dry land. The bears limit their activities, and they try to keep cool by staying on shady north-facing slopes, resting on snowdrifts, and excavating and retreating into snow caves or earth dens. Polar bears shed in summer, replacing their thick, insulating winter coat with a thinner one. The bears enter a lethargic state that some biologists refer to as "walking hibernation." They survive largely on their fat reserves. When they can, they eat carrion, lemmings, voles, gulls' eggs, and molting waterfowl. There are old records of bears eating fish, but modern observers have not seen that behavior. Polar bears—the most predaceous of all bears—occasionally consume grasses and crowberries, and some exhibit a fondness for kelp, perhaps for trace minerals the seaweed may contain.

4

Social Behavior and Territoriality

Unlike wolves, bears do not group together in packs. Rather, they are solitary, wide-ranging animals that encounter each other in a variety of situations and settings: when searching for food sources and feeding; locating mates and breeding; taking care of offspring; dispersing into new territories as young adults; and in the case of some polar bears in summer and early autumn, resting on land while waiting for the sea to ice over again.

Communication and the Social Hierarchy

Because they are large and powerful, bears could seriously injure each other if, whenever two individuals came into conflict, an actual physical struggle took place. Instead, bears, like most animals, use a series of communication displays—threat and appeasement signals that help them sort out dominance and submissiveness before a confrontation can escalate into a full-blown fight. Bears communicate with body movements, postures, and facial cues, most of which resemble those employed in social situations by the canids, including wolves. By varying the sequence and intensity of those signals, bears can send different messages.

A bear wanting to assert or establish its dominance over another bear will make a direct approach toward its rival. In reaction to such a challenge, a subordinate animal will back up, move aside, walk off, or run away. A dominant bruin tries to make itself look as large as possible, standing with its chest expanded and its head held high; a subordinate bear will drop its gaze, turn sideways or face away from its opponent, or sit or lie down.

To send a direct threat, a bear lowers its head while staring and lays its ears flat. It may also show its teeth. The vast majority of confrontations are settled through threat and appeasement. But if, after exchanging similar signals, neither of a pair of competitors backs down, the animals may fight. They advance toward each other, walking steadily or lunging forward in an out-and-out charge. They may lock their jaws together and try to wrestle each other to the ground. They may bite hard and trade blows with their front paws. At any stage in the conflict, either bear usually has the option of conceding the other's dominance and stopping the fight by adopting a posture of submission, backing off, and walking or running away.

During confrontations, grizzlies growl and roar; sometimes they rage so vociferously that they can be heard more than a mile away. Some wildlife biologists assert that black bears do not growl. Blacks express themselves through a variety of other sounds, however, including huffs, snorts, bawls, moans, and gurgles. They snap their jaws together rapidly, making ominous popping sounds. A black bear may cock back one front paw, as if ready to strike. It may smack the ground or some nearby object, such as a tree trunk, to make a loud, startling noise. Black bears are particularly good at bluffing. Mother black bears may charge at animals threatening their cubs, or those that they simply perceive to be a threat, including humans. Very seldom do the charges end in contact.

Black bears have larger ears relative to head size than grizzly bears, probably because black bears dwell in the forest, where the light is dimmer than in the grizzly's open-country domain and a bear's ears need to be large to express the animal's intentions. The ears of a black bear cub become adult size before the rest of the body is fully grown, helping an inexperienced youngster communicate social messages—including appeasement signals—more clearly. Black bears are more vocal in general than grizzly and polar bears, which evolved in more open settings where visibility is good and probably communicate more with visual cues than with sounds.

In a local population, each bear has a rank within a social hierarchy based on its age, gender, reproductive status, and individual temperament. In any given species and population—whether black bears in Florida, grizzlies in Montana, or polar bears in Alaska—the males are larger than the females. This size imbalance is known as sexual dimorphism; among mammals, it is most pronounced in bears, weasels, and cats. Humans also show sexual dimorphism, though usually to a lesser extent. Grizzly and polar bear males often weigh twice as much as females. In black bears, mature boars are 50 to 70 percent heavier than sows.

Big boars walk around among lesser bears in a fairly unconcerned fashion, secure in their size and strength and therefore their position of dominance. The largest males throw their weight around, staking out the best fishing spots and berry bushes, and appropriating the kills of smaller bears. The bigger a male becomes, the easier it is for him to dominate other male bears and ultimately advance his own genes by claiming and mating with a greater number of females.

Two polar bears wrestling off the shore of Hudson Bay. Bears may wrestle to establish dominance and find their place in the social hierarchy.

The roar of a grizzly bear can sometimes be heard from over a mile away.

One rung down on the social ladder from the big boars are sows with cubs. Mother bears are feisty in defense of their young, and other bears usually avoid them, with the occasional exception of large males, which may kill and eat the cubs if given the chance. Ranked slightly lower than females with cubs are adult males that are smaller than the dominant boars. These smaller, younger males may get to do some breeding, especially in populations with an abundance of females. Subadults of both sexes, including two- and three-year-olds, defer to adults, and young cubs occupy the lowest social stratum.

Old boars often carry scars on their heads, necks, shoulders, and forelimbs; they may be missing an ear or have a broken canine tooth. Despite the behaviors designed to minimize confrontation, bears sometimes fight, occasionally to the death. The battles usually take place during breeding season between two fairly equally matched males vying for the same female. Or a young male may trail after a pair of courting bears and then be unable to escape when the bigger, stronger male turns on him. The violence can be astonishing. In Canada's Jasper National Park, after a large male grizzly severely mauled and killed a smaller one, an autopsy revealed eighty-nine puncture wounds in the dead bear's body; his spleen stuck out through a hole in his abdomen, there was a 2-inch rent in his chest, his rib cage was smashed, one shoulder was broken, his neck was dislocated, and his skull was crushed.

The social hierarchy of bears is flexible, based on the reproductive state and physical condition of each individual and the food resources that are immediately available. A mature male grizzly may vigorously drive off other bears from a moose carcass he has sniffed out in spring, but he may let another bruin edge in closer or even take over his favorite fishing spot after he has satisfied his appetite during a late-summer salmon run. A pregnant or nursing female may answer the nutritional demands of her body with behaviors that are considerably more assertive than when she is shepherding about a pair of nearly grown cubs. And individual bears have different levels of tolerance toward their fellows: like humans, some bears are grouchy and others are more even-tempered.

Bears communicate in ways other than by expressing dominance and submission. The cubs of all species hum contentedly while nursing and cry out like children when they are in pain or afraid. A mother black bear can send her cubs scurrying up a tree with an explosive *huff*, then call them down again with a couple of grunts. Bears also leave messages in their urine, which contains sex hormones that other bears detect using their sense of smell; by rubbing their bodies against the rough bark of trees to leave a scent signal; and by physically marking trees.

Such trees are known as marker trees, bear trees, challenge trees, scratching trees, or rub trees. They are located next to trails, waterways, and ridgelines, along corridors followed by numbers of bears. A bear will pick out a prominent tree and use its claws and teeth to tear off a section of bark, opening up a prominent wound. It may rub its neck, back, or rump against the trunk, leaving hairs on any sap or resin that oozes out of the wound. The bear

may break off a nearby limb. These highly visible markings, most biologists believe, are not meant to serve as No Trespassing signs or mark off an individual's exclusive territory. Rather, they are advertisements. By rubbing against a tree, a bear leaves traces of its body odor, telling other bears that it is in the neighborhood. Both males and females mark trees. Odors left by males may stimulate females to enter estrus, the condition of being ready to breed. Most marking takes place during the early-summer breeding season, but bears also mark at different times of the year. Bears also mark telephone poles, trail signs, old fenceposts, cabins, and other man-made structures. Often the same tree or signpost is marked by several or many bears.

Biologists and naturalists once believed that dominant bears reached as high as they could on a tree to leave their mark in order to demonstrate their great size. This technique was supposed to intimidate smaller bears, which, when they happened upon the calling card of a boss bear, would leave and never come back. But often bears use their jaws to mark trees while keeping all four feet on the ground. Sometimes they climb partway up a tree to mark it. And if a marker tree or other habitual signpost falls over, bears may still mark it by lying down and rubbing against it.

Bears use urine to scent-mark within their home ranges. They straddle shrubs, tufts of grass, or saplings and urinate while walking over the obstructions. All three species of North American bears engage in this scent-marking behavior.

An ongoing flow of signals is extremely important to bears and to their social network and life habits. If the flow stops, the results can sometimes be deadly. When early grizzly researchers in Yellowstone National Park drugged a five-year-old female and she collapsed onto the ground, an adult male grizzly, observing her incapacitation, rushed up and killed her. People have seen cubs feeding on the carcass of their mother within a few hours of the adult's death.

One of the most intriguing ursine social situations occurs when the ice melts in summer on Canada's Hudson Bay and the resident polar bears come ashore. Large adult males settle onto headlands and small islands, which can be reached with the least expenditure of energy and offer cooling breezes blowing in off the open water. Subadults, both male and female, remain close to the shore in places not occupied by adult males. Adult females with young trek inland up to 25 miles, returning to the same areas in which they gave birth to their cubs during winter, inside dens. Scientists suggest that this movement pattern lets young female cubs learn where to go when it is time

Bears use their teeth and claws to mark trees, utility poles, trail signs, and human structures such as sheds. Often a marker tree is situated next to a well-used trail, where other bears can see it and contribute their own marks. A bear also may rub against a marker tree, leaving traces of its body odor, telling other bears that it is in the area and, in breeding season, advertising for a mate.

for them to deliver cubs of their own. Also, the mothers shift inland to stay away from adult males, which might kill the cubs.

As winter approaches, adult and subadult polar bear males gather on points of land, waiting for the bay to freeze over. During aerial surveys, biologists have observed 50 to more than 120 bears in certain locales, particularly a narrow spit of land extending out into the bay near Cape Churchill. The bears form into small groups, with three to a dozen or more individuals resting close to one another. The groups are fluid; individuals often leave one assemblage and join another. There are no food resources for which to compete (the bears are living off the body fat they accumulated during the previous spring and winter), and mating isn't an issue: the breeding season doesn't begin until the following April, and the bears' testosterone levels are at their lowest for the year.

As they wait, the bears play. They pair up, with two individuals of comparable size squaring off against each other—although sometimes a small bear will take on a large one, and groups of three and four also may come together. The bears tackle each other. They roll about, wrestling and chewing on each other's heads and necks, sometimes roughly enough to draw blood. Standing on their hind legs, they bat at each other with their massive forepaws and try to push and shove their opponent down. Most of their motions are deliberate and constrained; the bears look almost as if they are fighting in slow motion.

Do the Hudson Bay polar bears get together to play, or do they play because they find themselves in close proximity and have nothing better to do? Some biologists suggest that the play sessions let a bear test his neighbors' strength and vigor, and help him figure out, in a nonviolent manner, just where he stands in the social hierarchy. Playing may also help a bear hone its

PLAY AMONG BEARS

Like people, bears are individuals. Some cubs are more playful than others, just as some adult bears occasionally will lapse into play while others keep stolidly to the ursine business of vacuuming up food. Although not as frisky as they were when but six months old, bears continue to play with their littermates. A bear may invite attention by approaching a sibling in a bouncy, floppy, loose-limbed gait, similar to the way one dog will solicit another to play. Adult male polar bears play together in summer, when they are not hunting and when their hormone levels are at an ebb. Some adult grizzly and polar bears go tobogganing: they launch themselves down a snow or ice field, turn around and climb back up, and scoot downslope again.

In general, the better fed a bear is, the more likely it is to channel time and energy into playing. At McNeil River State Game Sanctuary in Alaska, adult grizzlies that have become sated after feeding on salmon sometimes pair off and play. Almost always, bears that are older than cubs play only with partners of the same sex. Sanctuary personnel have reported play among bears as old as eighteen years, including a few instances when an adult female and an adult male played together.

ability to assess the size and strength of other males. When the bears meet again on the ice in April and May while competing for females, they can better judge each other and avoid fights that might cause injury or death.

Home Ranges

The home range of any animal must be large enough to let the creature feed itself and any offspring, and come in contact with an individual of the opposite sex so that it can mate. A bear has a large home range compared with, say, a snowshoe hare. Whereas a hare can fulfill its life's needs on 20 acres, a bear might require 20 square miles. The home ranges of bears vary in size, depending on the species, sex and breeding condition of the individual, quality of the habitat, and reliability and location of key food sources.

Bears get to know their home ranges intimately. They discover and remember places where food is abundant and water sources where they can drink and wade or swim in summer to keep cool. They learn where potential dens are located. And between key habitat features, they find travel corridors, such as game trails, ridgetops, brushy areas bordering streams and rivers, woods edges, and wetlands margins.

Black and grizzly bears often travel on networks of trails threading through their home ranges. These trails make it easier for the bears to negotiate thickets and swampy or wooded terrain. The paths can also provide a bear with clues as to neighboring bears' movements and whereabouts. Marker trees, urine, and scents and odors that linger on frequently used trails advertise which individual bears have recently shuffled through, letting another bear decide whether to stay on the trail or alter its travel route to avoid a confrontation. If, for instance, a sow with young cubs detects the presence of a large male, she may head in a different direction to ensure her offspring's safety, since boars sometimes kill and eat cubs.

Of the three North American *Ursus* species, blacks generally have the smallest home ranges. In the predominantly oak forests of northeastern Pennsylvania, where state game commission biologists have intensively studied radio-collared black bears for more than three decades, the home ranges of females average 15 square miles and are 3 to 8 miles in diameter. Females with newborn cubs have smaller ranges that gradually expand as the cubs become more mobile. Sows whose young have recently dispersed and that are ready to breed again have larger ranges. The home range of a mature male will overlap those of several breeding females. In Minnesota, researcher Lynn Rogers found that some males shift about over areas encompassing all or parts of as many as fifteen females' ranges. This pattern, with females having smaller ranges than males, whose ranges include those of a number of breeding-age females, holds true for all North American bears and for many other wild creatures as well.

In the Brooks Range of Alaska, the typical female grizzly has a home range of 133 square miles; the average male's home range is 520 square miles, or almost four times as large. The home ranges of grizzlies along Alaska's salmon-rich coast are considerably more compact: a male may thrive on only 2 percent of the area required by a boar in the Brooks Range, and a given coastal locale may support one to two grizzlies per square mile. The high country of Yellowstone National Park and the surrounding mountains support a grizzly on every 20 to 40 square miles; the North Fork of the Flathead River, just west of Glacier National Park in Montana, is a richer ecosystem that in some areas supports one grizzly per 5 to 10 square miles.

Polar bears can have vast ranges, with some individuals traveling across 20,000 square miles in a single year. The largest polar bear home range ever documented exceeded 104,000 square miles—an area the size of Colorado. (Some biologists have wondered whether such a far-flung territory can be considered a home range, or simply the wanderings of a footloose individual.) In an Alaskan study, the average home range of a single polar bear was found to be forty-five times larger than the total area of Great Smoky Mountains National Park in Tennessee, which is home to 400 black bears.

Just as bears' social hierarchies are flexible and dynamic, so, too, are their ranges. In a year of abundant food—acorns in the eastern woods, buffaloberries in the Yukon, ringed seals in the Northwest Territories—bears may require only small home ranges. In years when food is scarce, their ranges may expand greatly.

The population density of bears can vary widely from place to place—again, depending largely on habitat quality and food availability. The great diversity in black bear populations illustrates this concept. Food-rich habitats in coastal Alaska and the oak woodlands of Pennsylvania can support eight to ten bruins per square mile. An island off the coast of Washington has a density of four individuals per square mile. One bear per square mile has been reported from parts of northern California, northern Maine, Montana, Arizona, and Tennessee. Marginal habitats in Minnesota and Michigan support 0.5 bears per square mile. Biologists located 0.7 bears per square mile in the best habitat in Yellowstone National Park and only 0.2 bears per square mile in the park as a whole.

Many animals stake out and guard individual territories, but that doesn't seem to be the case with polar bears, grizzlies, and most black bears. Because bears' home ranges are so large, patrolling and defending them would require an enormous expenditure of time and energy. Studies in Minnesota, Montana, and Alberta, however, suggest that some adult female black bears defend territories by aggressively driving off other sows, at times even killing them. In those areas, home ranges may be small enough to defend. And perhaps the females gain enough benefits from having the exclusive use of a territory—for feeding, breeding, and raising cubs—to justify spending the energy needed to defend the territory and risking serious injury in trying to repel or slay a rival.

When bears damage crops or otherwise annoy or frighten people in their ongoing search for food, wildlife specialists may need to catch them, usually with a steel culvert trap mounted on a set of wheels, and translocate them to remote areas. But bears have a strong homing instinct. In Pennsylvania, biologist Gary Alt found that he needed to transport a nuisance black bear farther than 40 miles from its home range to prevent its returning; less than that and the bear would be back within two weeks. Once Alt released a bear from a culvert trap and followed the bruin on foot. The bear ambled along for a ways, stopped, stood rigidly, and held its head forward and level with the ground. Planting its hind feet, it sidestepped with its front feet, pivoting its body like a compass needle. After making two circles, it headed straight for home. Biologists have found that adult bears are more apt to return home than subadults; if the distance is great, females with cubs are less likely to travel home than solitary females. Pennsylvania bears that are translocated farther than 100 air miles rarely return.

Other bears have made it home over greater distances. An adult male black bear in Michigan returned to his home territory after being transported by air for 156 miles. Removed 171 miles from her Yukon home, a female grizzly was back at the original capture site three days later. In some cases, translocated grizzlies are killed by resident bears in the areas to which they have been taken. Among grizzlies, subadults and sows with young have the lowest survival rates after translocation.

5

Breeding and Cubs

North America's terrestrial bears, the black and grizzly, usually mate in late spring to early summer, from around late May until July, with the peak of breeding taking place in June in most locales. (A sow that has lost her cubs may go into heat and breed as late as September.) The polar bear breeds earlier in the year, in April and May.

Most female black bears become sexually mature and breed when they are three and a half years old, and a few have been documented to breed at age two and a half. Female grizzly and polar bears mature sexually at four and a half, although grizzly sows in poor-quality habitats may not mature until age seven or eight. Male bears become able to breed at about the same age as females, but generally they do not take part in mating for several more years, or until they have become big enough to compete for sows with other mature males.

Courtship and Breeding

Well before the breeding season begins, when black and grizzly bears are still in their winter dens, the testicles of the males increase in size and begin to produce sperm. In late spring, the males start roaming through their territories, checking whether the females are without cubs and are coming into heat, or estrus—that is, whether they are ready to breed. Black and grizzly males follow trails habitually used by bears of both sexes. They sniff at places where females have bedded down and where they have urinated, trying to detect the presence of hormones that signal a sow going into estrus. Once a male locates a female, he stays near her for a short period. If he determines that she is in estrus, he begins following her closely. If she is not yet in estrus, he moves on in search of another sow. A male may check on as many as five females in one day.

As they enter estrus, females may wander a bit themselves. When studying black bears in Minnesota, biologist Lynn Rogers found that a female in estrus took less time to complete a circuit of her home range than one that was not. One estrous female ambled through her territory in a third of the time it normally took her. Repeatedly traveling through her home area increases the odds that a female will hook up with a mate. She will usually follow well-used paths, leaving frequent dribbles of urine behind her.

A sow remains in estrus for about three weeks. Her vulva, the external part of her sex organs, swells noticeably. One or more males may trail her, waiting for her to become receptive to mating. Dominant boars keep closer to an estrous sow than do lesser males. Rival males may fight: in Minnesota, Rogers recorded continuous battles lasting up to four minutes, with combatants trampling down vegetation and leaving behind clumps of fur. A male grizzly may try to herd an estrous female into an isolated area, such as a

A male black bear (left) resting with a cinnamon-phase female. An estrous sow may initially resist a male's advances, but she will eventually accept his presence.

small mountain valley, where she will be less apt to come in contact with other males. Male polar bears also sometimes sequester breeding females by keeping them in small bays and on hillsides away from areas of sea ice frequented by other bears.

At first, because her instincts tell her to avoid a potential predator, a female may flee from a large male. She may charge at him and try to drive him off. She may bite or lash out with a paw, but rarely does her suitor respond in kind. He continues to follow and wait; over time, the female will accept his advances. When courting, a male and female may chew on each other's heads and necks, nuzzle, and wrestle. During a three- to five-day period in the middle of her estrus, the female will stand still and allow the male to copulate with her. The male mounts the female from behind, his forelegs clasping her around the middle, in the manner of dogs. A pair will copulate for an average of twenty to thirty minutes, but sometimes as long as an hour.

A male may mate with a female repeatedly over several days before moving on in search of another sow. A dominant male may mate with several females. Over the course of her estrus, a female may breed with more than one male, which can result in a litter of cubs sired by different fathers. Pennsylvania biologist Gary Alt monitored one female black bear who mated with three separate males in an hour and a half. Scientists believe that promiscuity on the part of both sexes enhances genetic diversity in bear populations, as well as upping the odds that an individual will find a fertile mate.

In some mammalian species, the females are spontaneous ovulators, releasing egg cells, or ova, spontaneously as part of their breeding cycle. In other species, the females are induced ovulators; they do not release eggs until they mate.

Spontaneous ovulators include deer, as well as many other animals. If no male is present when a doe deer ovulates, her unfertilized eggs die within a few days and are flushed out of her reproductive system. Later, after a certain number of days have passed, the doe's ovaries release eggs again. This cycle continues until the female is bred and becomes pregnant. Spontaneous ovulators that are prey animals copulate for short periods; it would be dangerous for them to suspend their vigilance during prolonged mating.

Females that are induced ovulators release eggs only after coming into direct contact with a male. In many species with induced ovulation, individuals are solitary and, depending on their body size and mode of existence, may range over large areas to feed themselves and any offspring. Many predators are induced ovulators, including small ones such as weasels and bats, and large ones such as pumas. Although scientists have not yet definitively proven that bears are induced ovulators, all of the evidence points in that direction.

In induced ovulators, the act of mating itself causes the female to ovulate. During copulation, the male's penis physically stimulates the female's vagina and cervix, triggering the production of hormones that result in eggs being released. To ensure that ovulation takes place and eggs become fertilized, each mating session lasts for an extended period of time. Males of mammalian species that reproduce through induced ovulation possess a baculum, a rod-like bone that runs the length of the penis. In a mature male black bear, the baculum is about 6½ inches long; in a large polar bear, it can be 9 inches. The baculum keeps the penis erect in lieu of blood engorgement and helps stimulate the female.

Another intriguing adaptation in bear reproduction is delayed implantation. After a female's eggs are fertilized, they divide and divide again until they become blastocysts, sixteen-cell structures that are hollow and about the size of a pinhead. At that point, they stop developing and go on hold. For about five months, they float in the female's uterus as she goes about the business of feeding and building up body fat.

If a sow can accumulate enough fat to get her through winter dormancy *and* sustain the development of embryos and nursing of young, then the blastocysts become attached to the uterine wall and resume developing. The stimulus for their attachment, or implantation, appears to be day length: when light and darkness reach a certain balance, the sow's brain releases hormones that cause implantation to take place. In Pennsylvania black bears, blastocysts become implanted between mid-November and early December. Although females may have mated at different times, all litters are born during the first four weeks of January. In grizzlies, implantation typically takes place in late November, and the females give birth in late January.

In autumn, pregnant sows put on extra weight. A Pennsylvania study found that black bears gain an average of 88 pounds in years when they are pregnant, compared with 24 pounds when they are not pregnant, implying that three to four times as much body fat is needed to get through a successful pregnancy and produce enough milk to nourish newborns. If a female does not accumulate enough fat by the time she enters her winter den, her ovaries stop releasing progesterone, a hormone that supports and maintains pregnancy, and the blastocysts dissolve. Delayed implantation offers an easy out from a pregnancy that would endanger a too-thin female. It also lets bears mate at a time when feeding isn't such a critical undertaking, when they are not busy gorging themselves on autumn foods to layer on the fat that will see them through winter.

Denning and Giving Birth

Pregnant sows enter their winter dens somewhat earlier than sows with cubs, and markedly earlier than male bears. While the mother bear hibernates, her embryos develop. After a month, the fetus is the size of a mouse. The actual gestation ends up being about two months, an extremely short period for an animal as large as a bear. At birth, black bear cubs are 8 to 10 inches long and weigh 10 to 20 ounces—about the size of a squirrel. Grizzly and polar bear cubs weigh 21 to 25 ounces. The birth weight of a bear cub is approximately 1/300 to 1/500 that of its mother; in contrast, a human baby generally weighs about 1/15 as much as its mother. A mother bear gives birth to young that are

At birth, black bear cubs are 8 to 10 inches long and weigh 10 to 20 ounces—about the size of a squirrel. Newborns have long, sharp claws, which they use to drag themselves through their mother's fur, homing in on the warmth radiating from her nipples.

smaller in relation to her own body mass than those of any other placental mammal; in essence, while nursing her cubs in the safety of the den, a sow is undergoing what some biologists term an external pregnancy.

Newborn bears are covered with fine, short fur through which the skin is clearly visible. Their eyes are tightly closed, their ears are tiny and budlike, and they lack teeth. As her cubs are born, their mother licks them clean and consumes the embryonic membranes and afterbirth. By eating these birth by-products, the sow recovers the nutrients they contain. She also keeps the den clean, eliminating odors that might attract predators that remain active in winter, such as wolves and large cats. Newborn cubs are helpless and poorly coordinated, but they can screech and wail loudly. Their thin fur, once it is dry, affords some insulation. They have long, sharp claws, which they use to drag themselves through their mother's fur, homing in on the warmth radiating from her nipples. The sow lies on her side so that the nursing cubs are cradled in the pocket of warmth created by her curved torso. The mother bear breathes into this enclosed space, further warming it.

Female black and grizzly bears have six nipples: two pairs on the chest and another pair in the groin area. Polar bears, which give birth to smaller litters than blacks and grizzlies, have four nipples, all on the chest.

Bear milk is rich, containing up to 33 percent fat (heavy whipping cream is about 30 percent fat; a human mother's milk is less than 4 percent fat), 11 percent protein, and 10 percent carbohydrates. It is high in calcium and iron; since the female does not eat or drink during hibernation, biologists speculate that these essential growth elements come from bone decomposition in the sow's body. Cubs typically nurse for short spells, up to ten minutes every several hours. Their mother wakens periodically and licks her cubs to stimulate their digestive processes and clean up their urine and feces. A hibernating sow probably conserves and recycles water by consuming her cubs' waste.

When nursing, cubs of all bear species make a loud humming or chuckling that has been likened to the cooing of pigeons. Bears are thought to be the only carnivores whose young emit this sound. The cubs' vocalizing may stimulate the hibernating female to release milk and remind her to keep her body positioned properly to allow the cubs to nurse.

Litter size varies greatly, depending on the species of bear, the mother's age and physical condition, and how much food is available in the environment where she lives. In Pennsylvania, one of the richest and most productive black bear habitats known, females give birth to litters with 1 to 5 cubs; the average is 2.7. Young females reproducing for the first time often give birth to a single cub, and older females have larger litters. The average age of sows that produce litters of 5 cubs is nine and a half years. (Those data are based on 642 litters observed by biologists during captures and winter den visits of 473 radio-collared bears between 1975 and 2003.) In some exceptional cases, female black bears have given birth to 6 cubs. In parts of Montana where food is less abundant and reliable than in moist, diverse Pennsylvania, black bear females average only 1.7 young per litter.

Mother bears often nurse in a sitting position. This black bear sow has twins; one of the cubs is black, the usual color for the species, and the other is cinnamon.

Female grizzlies breeding for the first time usually have a single cub. As in black bears, when a sow grizzly grows older and larger—and more experienced at finding food—she tends to produce a greater number of cubs in each litter. The peak of reproduction in female grizzlies occurs from age eight to seventeen, although many females do not survive that long, particularly in areas where the bears are hunted. Overall, grizzlies probably average 2 cubs per litter. Some females have given birth to as many as 5, and there's a record of a Canadian sow delivering 6 cubs. Again, differences in habitat quality lead to a great variation in the reproduction rate: grizzlies in the salmon-rich forests of coastal Alaska average 2.5 cubs per litter, and those in sparsely vegetated mountainous habitat in the Yukon average 1.7 cubs per litter.

The grizzly has one of the lowest reproductive rates of all North American land mammals, but the polar bear is even less prolific. Some studies suggest that a female living in marginal habitat may give birth to only one or two litters in her lifetime. In the Canadian Arctic, female polar bears average 1.8 young per litter.

The polar bear's reproductive strategy is keyed to its annual cycle within the rigorous arctic environment. Because polar bears can hunt seals during winter, they are not forced to hibernate on account of food shortages. Pregnant females den specifically to give birth to their cubs in a stable, relatively sheltered environment. Beginning in September or October, the females leave the pack ice and come ashore in coastal areas and on islands. On the shores of Hudson Bay, sows that have waited out the brief summer on land remain where they are and allow winter's snows to accumulate around them.

Female polar bears dig their dens in deep snowbanks. They tunnel inward and downward for several yards, then hollow out an oval chamber about 6 feet in diameter and 3 to 5 feet high. The snow above the chamber, which may become 10 feet deep, helps insulate the lair. When scientists inserted a probe through the roof of one maternity den, they found that temperatures inside hovered between 27 and 36 degrees F; outside temperatures ranged from –22 degrees to 14 degrees. On some days, the air inside the den was 60 degrees warmer than outside.

Throughout the winter, the walls and ceiling of a maternity den may repeatedly melt and refreeze, until the resulting ice begins to block the exchange of gases. If the inside air gets too stuffy, a sow may excavate a new side chamber or scrape at the ice with her claws; both practices promote oxygen infiltration. Some snow dens have ventilating holes in the ceiling, either scratched by the female's claws or melted by her body heat. In southern parts of the polar bear's range, females may dig into the tundra and create earthen dens much like those of grizzlies.

Biologists have identified at least seventeen major core denning areas across the circumpolar range of the polar bear, in the former Soviet Union, Norway's Svalbard Archipelago, Greenland, and northern Canada. In some core areas, female bears den surprisingly close to one another. In Svalbard, researchers documented concentrations of thirty-one dens per square mile.

On Russia's Wrangel Island, six dens lay within a 359-square-yard tract. Because females usually den in the areas where they were born, concentrations of breeders may represent older females and their mature offspring.

About 2,000 polar bears live in Alaska, where females give birth to cubs in dens they dig in the snow on top of the sea ice. Scientists believe that in the past whalers and native hunters supplied with firearms by traders killed off bears that denned on the mainland. Either the remaining bears shifted to the ice or those that traditionally had denned on the ice were the only ones to survive. The sea ice is a less stable environment than the land. Large areas of ice can drift on ocean currents, carrying bears to areas where prey is scarce; and the ice can break up, forcing females and their offspring to leave the den before the cubs have grown large enough to withstand winter's cold and winds. As long as hunting pressure continues along the coast of northern Alaska, it is unlikely that *Ursus maritimus* will reestablish denning areas on land.

For more about denning in general, see the following chapter.

Development of Cubs

About four weeks after birth, the cubs' eyes open, although their vision is weak even at two months of age. Their first coat of real fur pushes forth. The teeth begin to erupt at around seven weeks. Within two months, well-nourished black bear cubs typically weigh 5 pounds. As the youngsters continue to grow and develop, they become increasingly alert and active within the den. They crawl about and may compete with each other during nursing, with an aggressive cub trying to claim "nursing rights" to several nipples and thus get more milk than its siblings.

Black and grizzly sows that have given birth to cubs are slow to leave the winter den. In early spring, food is scarce, and a sow would burn up many calories trying to find sustenance. The weather is often raw and cold. If cubs were taken outside too soon, they would need to keep their bodies fueled to stay warm, and the only way they could do that would be through nursing, which would further cut into their mother's already depleted energy reserves. It makes biological sense for the family to stay in the den, in a protected, relatively warm setting, for as long as they can.

By the time their mother leads them out into the bright world in spring, black or grizzly bear cubs, by now three to four months old, are able to walk along behind her. When they emerge from the den, black bear cubs can weigh up to 10 pounds; grizzly cubs are somewhat heavier.

After vacating the den, most bears remain in the near vicinity for a week or two. Mothers and young cubs may remain quite close to the den for as long as a month. They sleep in a day bed and sometimes they crawl back inside the den for brief periods.

When they first leave the den, cubs are a bit wobbly on their legs, but they can run, and black bear cubs can climb a tree if danger threatens. A mother black bear often escorts her young to a large hemlock or pine. The evergreen's

Young bears such as these two grizzly cubs tend to be lively and playful.

foliage provides some shelter from the elements, and the youngsters can shinny up the trunk in an emergency. The sow heads off to look for food and may be absent for several hours at a stretch. Sometimes her youngsters climb into the tree and rest, stretched out on a limb.

Cubs are full of energy, full of play. They wrestle with each other, launch surprise attacks, bite (but not too hard), kick, box, and cuff. A cub may play on its own, somersaulting or flopping onto its back and lying there rocking back and forth or fiddling with its toes. It may do battle with a tussock or stump. It may attack a stick or stone or bone, chew on the toy, drop it, walk away, turn and stalk and pounce. The biologist Stephen Herrero writes in *Bear Attacks* of seeing two bear cubs climb a sapling: "Their combined weight bent the tree to near the ground, where one cub hopped off and the other was catapulted up as the tree straightened. Soon both cubs were up the tree again to repeat the sequence." Most play sessions last for a few minutes at a time. A mother bear may join in and play with her offspring, especially if she has only one cub.

Watching a litter of black or grizzly cubs, one can only conclude that young bears play for the sheer fun of it. But play also confers biological advantages. All of that climbing and tumbling and pushing and pulling spurs the development of healthy bones and muscles. Those mock attacks on sticks and stumps, those stalks and pounces and free-for-alls, presage the adult activities of hunting, catching, and killing prey. Play strengthens the bond between a mother and her young, making her more attentive to her cubs, more apt to nurture, teach, and protect them. And playing lets cubs and youngsters learn the ursine "language," those key vocal and behavioral cues that convey aggression and appeasement, dominance and submission.

Both black and grizzly cubs may begin to feed right away on solid foods—perhaps buds and insects—but they will rely chiefly on their mother's milk for several more weeks. As cubs grow and develop, their innate curiosity may lead them to discover new food items, when they pick something up and manipulate and taste it. But the main way they learn is by watching their mother. When a sow flips over a rock and uncovers a meal of grubs or ants, the young remember. When a female grizzly digs out and kills a ground squirrel or a marmot, her cubs develop a taste for rodents. They learn that certain smells and noises make the sow cautious and other scents or sounds frighten or attract her. The wealth of experiences that cubs accrue during this formative period will help them survive when they finally leave the family group and strike out on their own.

During their first spring and summer, cubs are never far from their mother. She keeps a close eye on them and responds promptly when they whine or squall. A female grizzly will defend her young instantly and fiercely. A black bear sow will send her cubs up a tree; she will remain close by and may charge toward anything or anyone she believes to pose a threat. When she advances toward a human, however, rarely will she complete the charge and make contact.

As summer proceeds, the family group travels through the female's range; when the cubs get stronger and more mobile, the family expands its movements. The sow feeds heavily, replenishing her fat stores and making up for the demands placed on her body by nursing. She stops periodically to let her young suckle, sitting down and leaning back, often with her eyes closed. When she decides the nursing period is over, often she simply stands up, dumping the cubs on the ground.

Young bears grow rapidly, particularly between the ages of six months and two and a half years; after that, their growth tails off, although most healthy bears generally continue to add size and weight throughout their lives. Growth rate and size depend on food availability. By their first autumn, grizzly cubs in the Yellowstone area usually weigh 60 to 70 pounds. In general, most grizzly youngsters weigh 75 to 100 pounds by this time. Across the species' range, black bear cubs are somewhat smaller, although in mast-rich hardwood forests, they may duplicate that 75- to 100-pound figure for grizzlies by denning time in late autumn. Biologists have documented some first-year black bear cubs weighing more than 140 pounds.

Young polar bears are born in December or January, and they grow even more rapidly, weighing 22 to 33 pounds by the time they leave the maternity den in March or April. At first the cubs stick close to the den entrance, playing and becoming accustomed to colder temperatures. If the female detects any danger, she quickly shepherds her litter back inside. She suckles her cubs six or seven times a day, for about fifteen minutes each session. She may scoop out a shallow pit and lie in it, letting the cubs rest on her abdomen, or she may sit and lean forward to let them nurse. When they are ready to leave the den for good, she leads them across the frozen tundra and onto the sea ice. Young cubs may ride on their mother's back when she swims. On the ice, the cubs trail behind her as she hunts for seals. She shares her prey with her young. By August, healthy cubs can weigh 100 pounds or more. They will den with their mother for one or two more winters and will continue to nurse until they are nearly two years old.

When female polar bears emerge from their dens with cubs in tow, they need quick access to reliable food sources, so most denning areas are located near major polynyas and lead systems. These fertile zones remain unfrozen in

Polar bear cubs generally stay with their mother until they are two and a half years old.

winter and produce abundant algae and plankton, which feed invertebrates that support fish, both of which attract seals and other marine mammals that polar bears prey on.

Cubs of all species face many perils. They die in accidents, falling out of trees and over cliffs, and getting caught in snow and rock avalanches. Some drown, and others are hit by vehicles. Cubs succumb to malnutrition and disease. Some are taken by predators, including pumas, wolves, coyotes, bobcats, golden eagles, and alligators. About a third of all black bear cubs die in their first year, most of them during their first six months. A study in Alaska found that 40 percent of grizzly cubs did not survive to age one and a half; in northern Canada, researchers documented up to 75 percent mortality in first-year grizzly cubs. Statistics from polar bears in the Hudson Bay region suggest that more than half of the cubs born there may perish before their first autumn.

Perhaps the biggest threat to cubs comes from adult male bears. In recent years, as researchers have conducted field studies of bears and other wildlife, they have come to realize that the killing of infants by adults of the same species is fairly common in the animal world. Biologists have observed this behavior in eagles, wolves, pumas, ground squirrels, tigers, lions, gorillas, chimpanzees, and many other species, including all three North American bears. In an Arizona black bear study, half of the cubs that died after leaving the den in spring were killed by adult males. John and Frank Craighead, the first scientists to systematically study the grizzlies of Yellowstone National Park, recorded four instances of males killing cubs. Researchers on Kodiak Island in Alaska watched a large male grizzly drive a sow and her cub up a steep snow slide. After climbing for thirty minutes, the exhausted cub stopped; the boar caught up to it, seized its head in his jaws, and shook it until it was dead. Then the male continued to follow the female, which retreated over a nearby ridge.

Scientists have several theories on why bears kill their own kind. A boar may eliminate cubs to promote breeding opportunities, since a female who loses her cubs stops lactating and soon goes into heat. He may simply see a cub as prey, since some boars eat the cubs they kill. When one bear kills another, it reduces the competition for limited food resources, which also may explain why sows occasionally attack and kill cubs belonging to other females.

Sows with cubs are careful to avoid male bears. When male grizzlies go on the prowl during the May–June breeding season, a sow may take her litter out onto a steep, treeless slope, far from the travel corridors frequented by most bears and with a good view of the surrounding terrain. If a male happens past, the female can watch him and retreat if necessary. Female polar bears lead their cubs away from floe edges and pack ice, where males often hunt, and conduct their own hunting in other areas.

Most sows are exemplary mothers, but in some rare instances, females abandon their own cubs. A black bear researcher in Arizona believed females sometimes abandoned the remaining cub in a litter of two after the first had been killed by predators or had died of some other cause. During one autumn in Utah, biologists located more than twenty black bear cubs wandering on their own. Food was scarce that fall, and the investigators speculated that to save their own lives, females had walked away from their young. Montana grizzlies have also abandoned their cubs. It is clear why a female facing a lack of food might leave a cub. More complex biological imperatives may also be at work. In grizzlies, for instance, a litter takes two and a half years to raise, whether that litter contains a single cub or four. In good-quality habitat, a female might increase her lifetime production of offspring by abandoning a lone cub, "gambling" that she would breed the following year and deliver a larger litter. Sacrificing a live cub—probably not as the result of a conscious decision, but through following some deep-seated instinct—might actually serve to advance the female's own genes.

Cubs that have been abandoned or whose mothers have been killed are not always doomed to death. Orphaned grizzly cubs as young as seven months have survived on their own. Black bear cubs orphaned when only five and a half months old have somehow gotten enough food, evaded predators, and found places to hibernate. In 1975 in Jasper National Park, Alberta, three grizzly cubs were orphaned during their first summer. When spotted again the following May, the cubs appeared to be healthy. That summer they fed together, eating grasses, roots, insects, and rodents, and they appropriated a marmot that a coyote had killed. Two of the cubs denned together over winter and remained with each other the following spring. In May, researchers captured the duo and outfitted them with radio collars. By October, the bears had almost doubled their weight. As subadults, the pair remained together for two more years before biologists removed their radio collars and ceased monitoring them.

Under normal conditions, cubs of the year enter the winter den and hibernate with their mother. In spring, the family emerges intact. The cubs learn from their mother where and how to find key early-spring foods. As summer progresses, the cubs continue to nurse, but less frequently. They wander farther away from the sow, and their increasing separateness does not bother her as it would have when the cubs were less than a year old. At times, they feed and even hunt on their own, sometimes at a considerable distance from their mother. Ian Stirling, the Canadian researcher, found that yearling polar bear cubs stayed within 1/3 mile of their mother, but by the time they were two and a half, they often would hunt as far as 1 1/4 miles away.

Black bear families break up when the cubs are about seventeen months of age, toward the end of their second summer. At this stage of life, they are referred to by biologists as subadults. Grizzly and polar bear cubs generally stay with their mothers for an additional year, the young being two and a half years old when the family dissolves. In the harsh, barren habitat of northern Alaska, some black bear cubs stay with their mothers for an extra year, until they become large enough to fend for themselves.

The breakup of a family can be gradual and undramatic, the cubs slowly drifting away from their mother over a period of days. Some mother bears chase their young off, charging at them repeatedly, sometimes even biting them, until they finally flee. In summer, the female usually comes into heat again, and when an adult male moves in to mate with her, he—or simply his presence—may drive her cubs away. Grizzly families usually break up in the early-summer breeding season. Most mothers become hostile toward their young after separation. In a Minnesota study, of fifty-one black bear family units that broke up during the breeding season, only one got back together again.

When black bear families dissolve, the yearlings separate from each other. Grizzly siblings have a stronger bond and often stay together for another year or two, frequently hunting as a team. They may share a den or they may den separately and then reunite in the spring. When they finally strike out on their own, most female cubs—both blacks and grizzlies—set up their own home ranges close to or within their mothers' territories, especially in rich habitats where food is plentiful. Young males leave their mothers' territories when they are one to four years of age, and they may travel 100 miles or farther before settling into a territory of their own.

6

Denning and Hibernation

Different animals react to the stresses of winter in different ways. Migratory birds shift south to warmer climates. Other birds, as well as mammals such as raccoons and opossums, hole up during bitter cold or deep snow and move about in more moderate weather in a near-continual search for food. Squirrels consume seeds and nuts they have hoarded. Deer eat whatever forage they can find while remaining fairly inactive, traveling little to avoid wasting calories that must be provided by the metabolizing of body fat.

Polar bears live in an environment where it is not usual for food to become scarce in winter, so they remain active, hunting for equally active warm-blooded prey through the long, dim arctic winter. Pregnant polar bear females den in winter to give birth to their cubs, however, and individuals of both sexes and all ages may resort briefly to snow dens when the weather is especially bad or the hunting is poor. But black and grizzly bears exhibit a strange and miraculous behavior for which bears are justifiably famous: they hibernate.

In winter, blacks and grizzlies enter a period of extremely limited activity, not because they cannot withstand cold, but because foodstuffs in the environment have become too scarce to fuel their large bodies. Some scientists quibble about whether bears actually hibernate, and indeed, many other creatures from frogs to woodchucks become much more sluggish in winter. Essentially, bears lapse into a deep, energy-conserving sleep during which they do not eat, drink, defecate, or urinate. Though this pattern fits the general definition of hibernation as an inactive or dormant state, some biologists prefer to call it winter sleep or winter lethargy.

What physiological factor tells a bear to stop feeding in autumn and enter the den that will be its home for the next two to seven months? Scientists

During winter, bears hibernate by lapsing into a deep, energy-conserving sleep during which they do not eat, drink, defecate, or urinate.

believe it is the amount of fat accumulated in a bear's body that ultimately leads the animal to den. But denning is far from an automatic behavior. Well-fed bears in zoos may not den. And wild bears that have the opportunity to keep on eating sometimes do so, not retreating to their dens until food supplies dwindle or the weather gets really bad. Individuals that have not put on sufficient fat may also keep hunting for food. Conversely, in years when acorn crops fail, eastern black bears may den early, since the gains from continuing to look for food do not exceed the amount of energy being spent. A bear that goes into its den with insufficient fat reserves may leave its shelter in the middle of winter and begin a desperate search for food. Bears that emerge at this time often are sick, old, or injured, or they are subadults that, owing to a lack of experience at finding food, were unable to layer on enough fat during the preceding autumn.

Bears may be remarkably lax about going into the den. If the weather stays warm, they may loll about in the vicinity of the lair, eating little or nothing and sleeping for hours on end. When researchers in Minnesota monitored a black bear female and her two cubs during late September, after almost all food sources had dried up, the bears spent more than twenty-two hours a day simply resting.

Montana biologist and author Douglas Chadwick notes in *True Grizz* that some adult grizzlies tarry outside in autumn, mainly "big, burly, and therefore cold-resistant males . . . making a good living off hunters' leavings—gut piles and the carcasses of animals fatally wounded but never tracked down." Chadwick suggests that hibernation in grizzlies is "a matter of energy intake versus energy output. As long as the balance stays favorable, a grizzly has no pressing need to dig into a hillside and snooze the cold months away." In some coastal habitats in southeastern Alaska, biologists have spotted grizzlies out and about during all months of the year. Some individuals dig dens but use them only for short periods, when the weather is bitter or when hunting and foraging are poor. In the Rockies, grizzlies occasionally leave their dens during midwinter thaws. And recent research suggests that black bears also may leave their dens for short periods in winter.

Among grizzly and black bears, pregnant females and sows with cubs are the first to den. Then come subadults, and finally mature males. In Yellowstone National Park, female grizzlies begin entering their dens during the fourth week of September, with 90 percent of sows denned by the fourth week of November; males den about two weeks later. Bears may begin denning any time from early October to early January, depending on where in North America they dwell.

Finding or Digging a Den

A bear may move several miles to reach a den site, which it probably checked out and committed to memory while traveling through its home range during summer. Bears remember several den sites. Individuals that are forced to leave a den in winter, after being disturbed by people or after the den becomes flooded or its ceiling collapses, often move straight to another den site. In New Hampshire, biologists found that black bears sometimes denned outside their normal territories when headed back home after extended autumn forays to areas with abundant food.

In most instances, bears den in places that are secluded, dry, and well drained, and where snow is likely to pile up in winter and not melt too early in spring; the snow offers added insulation when it lies on top of the den. Grizzlies often site their dens on slopes at high elevations. Snow accumulates more deeply at these loftier heights, and on many days the temperature remains warmer there than at lower levels, where cold air tends to pool during calm weather. Biologists have not found evidence that either black or grizzly bears dig snow dens as polar bears do.

Grizzly bears, diggers par excellence, use their powerful shoulder muscles and sturdy claws to carve dens out of the ground. A grizzly may start its excavation beneath a large rock or tree root. Some grizzlies living on the far northern tundra dig their dens under clumps of alders and willows, whose dense, interwoven root systems stabilize the soil and keep the dens' ceilings from collapsing in spring. The shrubs also break up the wind, which encourages snow to collect. When a researcher in Canada's Northwest Territories studied grizzly dens beneath thickets, he found that the snow depth above the dens averaged 30 inches, while snow on nearby open ground lay only 6 inches deep.

A typical grizzly den has a single tunnel, usually 3 to 6 feet long though sometimes much longer, up to 15 feet or more. It leads to an egg-shaped chamber roughly 6 feet in length, 4 to 5 feet wide, and 3 feet high. A sleeping area of that size is sufficient for a bear to turn around in. It need not be larger, and a compact den minimizes the volume of dead air space that the bear's body heat must keep warm. The sleeping area may be slightly elevated, trapping heat and providing drainage if the roof leaks.

Up to a ton of dirt and rocks may be excavated during the digging of a den, creating a conspicuous mound near the opening. Many grizzlies dig horizontally into slopes, which may be quite steep. Generally it takes a grizzly five to seven days to dig its den. During the construction phase, the bear rests in a day bed nearby. Grizzlies also den in the hollow bases of large trees and in rock cavities, some of which have been used by generations of bears. A grizzly may line its sleeping chamber with dry grasses, leaves, small evergreen boughs, or other plant matter. Rarely, grizzlies use surface nests, sleeping outside all winter on grasses and other insulating materials placed directly on the ground. The bear's fur and thick layer of fat provide insulation, and its body build—rotund with short limbs—favors heat retention.

In some areas, up to half of all black bears do not bother with digging dens—perhaps in part because, with their short, curved claws, blacks are much less adept at excavating than grizzlies. Surface dens are fairly common in the southern half of the black bear's range—the Carolinas, Georgia, Florida, and Louisiana—and are less common in places where winters are longer and colder. Adult boars are much more likely to hibernate above ground than are subadults and females. Yet females may also nest on the surface, and some even give birth to cubs in such exposed situations.

An in-ground den has the advantage of radiating the earth's latent heat to its occupant. In sandy soils, such as those found in formerly glaciated parts of New England and the Upper Midwest, black bears readily dig dens. They tend not to be as extensive as those of grizzlies, averaging about 19 cubic feet in volume, roughly 3 feet long, 3 feet wide, and slightly more than 2 feet high. Black bears sometimes enlarge the burrows of woodchucks, foxes, coyotes, or badgers. They also may den inside shallow caves or rock crevices; in hollow logs or depressions at the bases of fallen trees; inside large brush piles; or on top of the ground in thickets of brushy or shrubby vegetation, such as blackberry, mountain laurel, or rhododendron, or in dense stands of immature spruce and balsam fir. Like grizzlies, blacks may drag together an insulating layer of leaves and grasses, mosses and bark, placing the material directly on the ground or arranging it inside an enclosed space. Even when black bears den in permanent sites, such as rock crevices and caves, it is rare for the same bear to use the same den for two consecutive winters. In areas with many

potential den sites, only about 5 percent of known bear dens are used two years in a row. Where den availability is low, the rate of reuse is higher. Switching dens each winter may serve to keep predators from learning their locations or minimize disease transmission among bears.

Sometimes dens get flooded. When this happens, a bear may shift to another den close by, or it may hastily build a nest of plant materials on top of the ground and sleep in the open until spring. Or it may return to its original den after the water recedes. Cubs have drowned when maternal dens flooded. Since bears are good learners, they probably choose better den sites as they grow older.

Tree cavities can make excellent dens. These voids come about after damage caused by a lightning strike or a limb bro-

Both black and grizzly bears may dig their winter dens beneath the roots of large trees. In-ground dens transmit the earth's latent heat to hibernating bears.

ken off by wind, ice, or wet snow opens a tree's interior tissues to wood-decay fungi. Over time, a tree will wall off a rotted area with new wood; sometimes a mature tree becomes little more than a cylinder of live wood enclosing a cavity. Since they're adept at climbing, black bears can ascend and enter rotted-out portions of the trunk high up in large trees—in some cases, 60 feet above the ground. Sometimes bears claw at cavity walls, dislodging punky wood chips, which then serve as bedding. Most tree cavities are secure, out-of-the-way places; they are dry and fairly well insulated, and they blunt the wind, resulting in an estimated 15 percent energy savings for a hibernating bruin. Often the entry holes to these hideaways are quite small. Tennessee researchers studying tree dens, used by many of the local black bears, found that the average entry portal was 12 by $21^{1/2}$ inches. Smaller bears—subadults and females—are the ones most able to fit into tree cavities.

Most den trees have a trunk 3 feet or more in diameter, which usually means that the tree is quite old—in some cases, more than three centuries old. Foresters and astute landowners leave large hollow trees standing to benefit bears and other cavity-using wildlife, including owls, woodpeckers, wood ducks, raccoons, squirrels, porcupines, and fishers. Black-gum is one tree that almost always becomes hollow when it reaches a great age; the species is common in the East from Maine to Florida. Black bears have also denned in cavities in yellow birch, red maple, and red oak.

Black bears have denned in some very odd places. One bruin located its winter lair on top of a muskrat house; others have burrowed into beaver dams. In northeastern Pennsylvania, a radio-collared sow and her cubs denned in a drainage culvert beneath an interstate highway; when heavy rains threatened, biologists sedated the bears and moved them to a dry den, where the family spent the rest of the winter. Black bears have also taken up winter residence in crawl spaces under people's houses and beneath wooden decks, often without the homeowners' knowledge. In the Pocono Mountains of Pennsylvania, bears often den in close proximity to humans: when someone builds a house 50 feet from a traditional den, it's likely that bears will keep on sleeping there if no one shoos them away.

Since bears neither urinate nor defecate inside the den, few odors arise to attract predators; observers have watched dogs walk past bear dens without scenting their occupants. Although most dens provide good shelter against the elements, they are not always predator-proof. Large male black bears have attacked and killed smaller bears in their dens—usually females, subadults, or cubs, but occasionally other adult males. In Alberta, a large female grizzly and her two yearlings followed the tracks in the snow of a mother black bear and her cubs. The grizzlies raided the blacks' den, killing the two cubs; the mother black bear survived the attack. In Alberta, Manitoba, Minnesota, and Michigan, bear researchers have found evidence of wolf packs killing denned black bears. Small bears that have squeezed into crevices and caves with tight, rock-bound entrances usually sleep safe from predators.

In the Den

Woodchucks, jumping mice, and ground squirrels are examples of mammals that, in winter, fall into a much deeper state of suspended animation than bears. A ground squirrel's heart rate drops from 500 to 600 beats per minute to around 25. Its metabolic rate decreases to 4 percent of normal. Its temperature sinks to within a degree or two of freezing. In its den, a ground squirrel lies tucked into a tight ball, its head between its legs, its furry tail wrapped around its body. The creature feels cold to the touch and does not respond if it is handled. As winter progresses, the rodent periodically wakes up, as often as once a week, going through a period of intense shivering and burning significant numbers of calories as its heart rate and temperature temporarily return to normal. Apparently restarting these vital processes is necessary for a ground squirrel to successfully make it through winter. During the waking periods, the squirrel urinates and may defecate; then it lapses back into hibernation.

Bears' dormancy lies on them like a thin blanket compared with the ground squirrel's shroud. A bear's heart, which normally beats forty to seventy times per minute, now beats eight to twelve times. The metabolic rate is halved in black bears, and in grizzlies it falls by one-quarter to one-third. The body temperature lowers by about 10 degrees or less: in the black bear, from summer's 99 to 101 degrees F to between 88 and 95; in the grizzly, from 99 degrees to 89 or 90. In a warm climate, as in Florida or Louisiana, a hibernating black bear may not fall completely asleep; in northern areas, bears do sleep soundly—but not so soundly that they can't be wakened. Mother bears have the highest temperatures. In Pennsylvania, according to bear biologist Gary Alt, pregnant females are the deepest hibernators, but once their cubs are born, the new mothers become the lightest sleepers.

Intrepid researchers who have entered the dens of hibernating black bears report that the bruins will rouse after being poked and prodded. If a bear is disturbed and decides to leave the den, its first movements may be awkward

ADOPTING CUBS

A sow's sense of smell is diminished during hibernation. Biologists take advantage of that fact to introduce orphaned cubs to black bear mothers. An orphaned cub is either tossed into the den or left just outside the den entrance. The sow groggily sniffs at the cub, then gathers it in and adds it to her litter. But once the mother emerges from the den in spring, she can tell from its odor that an orphaned cub is not her own and generally kills and eats it. To get around this instinctual behavior, biologists sometimes sedate a potential foster mother, dab her nostrils with a highly aromatic cold preparation, and coat the cub with the same medicine. Waking up, the sow licks off all the cubs around her—the orphan included—and by the time the preparation has worn off, the orphan carries enough of the sow's or her cubs' odors that it is accepted as one of the family.

and slow, because blood flow to the muscles is reduced during hibernation. (The blood is shunted into vital organs as part of the process of rationing stored fat reserves.)

Biologists occasionally crawl into dens to tranquilize black bears, with the goal of changing their radio collars, drawing blood samples, taking weights and other measurements—even depositing orphaned cubs with new mothers. If a black bear wakes up before it can be sedated, it will usually stay inside the den, or if it leaves, it will simply run away. It is best to avoid disturbing bears in winter, however, because leaving its den can cause a bear to lose over 50 percent more of its body weight than it otherwise would, a development that can prove fatal to an animal with limited fat reserves. Grizzlies do not sleep as soundly as black bears. They also are notably grouchier and may charge people who get too near their dens. Despite these behavioral differences, the physical details of hibernation are believed to be the same or very similar in both blacks and grizzlies.

Scientists have identified a protein in the blood of hibernating mammals, including woodchucks, ground squirrels, and bears, which they call hibernation induction trigger (HIT). When injected into ground squirrels in summer, HIT causes the rodents to become drowsy and fall asleep. Oddly, it even has a similar effect on monkeys. HIT appears to be the actual substance that starts the hibernation sequence.

While a bear is hibernating, the hormone leptin is secreted by the animal's fat cells. Leptin circulates in the blood; it affects the appetite centers in the brain, helping suppress the desire to eat. In spring, leptin levels fall and a bear's appetite returns.

The blood of black bears has a greater number of smaller red blood cells than does the blood of dogs and humans. More and smaller blood corpuscles mean a greater surface area of cells per a given volume of blood. Perhaps this increased surface area promotes a more efficient exchange of oxygen and carbon dioxide.

Hibernating bears stay alive by slowly metabolizing their fat, which can be 5 inches thick in black bears and 10 inches thick on the back of a big, well-fed grizzly. A bear burns around 4,000 calories per day while denning. Bears gradually lose weight through the winter: 15 to 30 percent of body weight in most bears, and up to 40 percent in females who give birth and nurse a litter of cubs. Grizzlies on Kodiak Island, off the coast of Alaska, regularly lose 100 pounds in winter.

The physiological details of hibernation are not completely understood, but science has revealed some of its aspects. When burning fat, mammals also metabolize small amounts of protein. The breakdown of protein produces a waste product, urea, a vehicle for getting rid of nitrogen. Under normal conditions, urea is filtered out of the blood by the kidneys and excreted in the urine; if it is not excreted, it builds up and causes urea poisoning, which can be fatal. A bear does not urinate while hibernating. Its kidneys remove urea from the blood, converting it into a nontoxic compound called creatine. Since it doesn't need to flush out wastes with urine, the bear conserves water. Water lost during lactation, by exhalation, or through the skin is replaced by water derived as a by-product of the breakdown of fat.

Although they are completely sedentary—curled up on the den floor in a non-weight-bearing position—bears do not incur bone loss, or osteoporosis, which afflicts people who are bedridden. And even though hibernating bruins use their muscles very little, their muscle mass does not decrease radically, as it would in a person confined to a wheelchair or hospital bed, or one who spends months orbiting the planet, weightless in a space station. In bears, nitrogen produced by the breakdown of protein is biochemically recycled into new replacement proteins, which help keep muscle tissues from wasting away. A bear's body also produces a specific acid that dissolves cholesterol formed during the metabolism of fat, so that the animal does not develop hardening of the arteries or gallstones, two afflictions that often strike humans who have too much fat in their diets.

In essence, bears have evolved to withstand the rigors of prolonged inactivity. As University of Vermont ecologist Bernd Heinrich suggests, a bear is "the ultimate enviable couch potato."

In different parts of the country, bears hibernate for differing amounts of time. Black bears in Florida sleep for two months or less (in southern Florida, some bears do not bother hibernating at all), and in North Carolina, for about three months. The hibernation period in study areas in New York, Pennsylvania, and Arizona is four to five months. In Maine, New Hampshire, Minnesota, and Idaho, black bears hibernate for five to seven months, and in the Yukon Territory, bears may hibernate seven months or even longer. The longest sleep verified for any bear occurred in southern Alaska, where a black bear hibernated for 247 days, or eight and a quarter months.

As might be expected, myths have grown up around animals that vanish into the earth in autumn, only to emerge again, fit and healthy, in spring. Some cultures held that bears died in the fall and were miraculously reborn the next year. Aboriginal peoples of North America, Europe, and Siberia thought that bears in the den licked and sucked on their paws for nourishment. Over winter, bears shed the outer layer of their foot pads, a process that takes several weeks or months. Sometimes pieces of these calluses are found in bear scats, which could have led people to conclude that they were taken in as nourishment. And perhaps they are indeed recycled for trace nutrients. Biologists in Minnesota have noted that bears that vacated their dens in late winter sometimes bled slightly from the feet when they scuffed their tender new pads on ice and snow.

Many people still believe the notion that before entering hibernation, a bear finds some moss or similar material and uses it to plug up its anus. A more sophisticated version of this belief has the bear eating indigestible items, such as resinous plant fibers, that compact to form an anal plug. Some people suppose that this plug prevents the bear from defecating during its denning period; in the spring, the bear cannot start eating again until it expels the plug. Long, hard, dry bear scats are sometimes found in spring, such as the one collected by an Alaskan biologist near the den of a large male grizzly: the dropping was 29½ inches long and 2 to 2¾ inches in diameter. Similar droppings have contained hair, grass, leaves, twigs, and other items that probably found their way into a bear's digestive tract when the bruin accidentally swallowed them while preparing its den or grooming itself or its cubs. The motility of a bear's bowels shuts down during hibernation, which can cause the contents of the lower intestine to compact. Once a bear leaves the den and starts roaming around in spring, the intestinal tract regains its motility and soon discharges its contents. Highly compacted, early-spring scats probably are the origin of the anal plug myth.

March, April, and May are the main months when bears leave their dens. A host of factors influence the exact timing when blacks and grizzlies shake off their torpor. If berry and nut crops were lean the previous autumn, bears may come out early; these individuals have burned up most of their fat reserves and must go looking for food. In the aftermath of bumper crops of soft and hard mast, bears may have enough body fat in reserve that they den longer into spring and come out closer to the time when new foods start becoming available.

Latitude, altitude, and temperature affect the timing of den emergence. Spring comes earlier to more southerly locations; to south-facing slopes in advance of north-facing declivities; and to valley floors ahead of mountains. In general, adult males are the first to leave the den, even though they were the last to enter hibernation in autumn. Then come subadults of both sexes and black bear females with year-old cubs or grizzly females with one- or two-year-old cubs. Finally, sows with newborns come blinking out into the sun. And a new cycle of ursine living begins.

7

Bears and Humans

Bear Science

Probably no other group of North American mammals has been studied as extensively as bears. Over the past forty years, scientists have learned more about bears than people had figured out in the preceding four centuries. They have debunked myths about bears. They have documented details of hibernation, feeding habits, prey preferences, home ranges, social interactions, and blood chemistry. They have figured out how to get wild mother bears to accept and raise orphaned cubs not of their own. They have examined black bears from Florida to Alaska, grizzlies in their Rocky Mountain and northwestern ranges, polar bears in the Arctic. This recent and thorough examination grows out of our fascination with bears, which, without a doubt, are among the most charismatic of the "charismatic megafauna," a term coined to describe particularly dramatic, fascinating, and beloved large animals.

Most extensive studies of bear biology and populations rely on capturing individual animals and marking them with ear tags or equipping them with radio collars. Biologists use two main types of traps to catch bears. One is a length of large-diameter culvert pipe welded to a wheeled trailer that can be towed from place to place. When a bear grabs a food bait attached to a trigger, a heavy gate slides shut, trapping the bear inside the pipe. To capture research subjects in roadless settings, biologists set foot snares made out of flexible aircraft cable. The cable is anchored to a tree; both the cable and a triggering device are concealed beneath soil and leaf litter. Everything from stale doughnuts to rotten fish can be used to attract a bear. Logs and sticks are arranged to guide the bruin's foot into the snare.

Caught in a snare, a black bear will usually struggle for a while, then give up and wait. When a human approaches, the bear will back away and perhaps cringe. A grizzly, on the other hand, will rage, tearing apart bushes and biting small trees into splinters. When humans arrive, the bear is likely to charge. Douglas Chadwick has seen grizzlies hit the end of a cable hard enough to turn a double somersault. "Injuries to the ankles and feet are not common," he writes in *True Grizz*, "but they occur, and a grizz held only by the toes may rip some off in its frenzy to be free." Trapped bears are immobilized with drugs delivered by a syringe mounted on a long stick or by shooting the animal with a dart.

The single most important technological tool aiding the study of bears is the radio collar. This device contains a battery-powered radio transmitter that sends a signal on a specific frequency. Using a receiver to take repeated readings on the collar's location, a scientist can closely chart the movement of a collared bear. (Or almost any other animal: transmitters, which keep getting smaller and lighter, have been clipped to turtles' shells and birds' wings, surgically implanted in the body cavities of otters, and glued to the carapaces of beetles.)

Nowadays, some collars come equipped with global positioning system (GPS) devices, allowing the constant, precise monitoring of an animal's location. Other collars have memory boards that store data electronically, such as changes in ambient temperature or the number of seconds that a subject animal is in motion during a given time span. After sedating the bear, biologists remove the collar, plug it into a computer, and download data that reveal shifts in temperature or exactly when the creature was active and inactive during the period in question. Most radio collars are designed to work for a few years and then drop off.

Some biologists have taken a less technological and more intimate approach to studying bears, recording close observations of the activities of individual animals. The first researcher to use this technique on bears was Lynn Rogers, who in the 1980s began studying a population of black bears on national forest land in northern Minnesota. Rogers habituated bears to his presence so that he could follow the animals as they went about their daily lives. The technique resembles the way researchers Dian Fossey and Jane Goodall became accepted by gorillas and chimpanzees, respectively, allowing them to make new and important observations about those primates and their behavior.

At first Rogers set up a feeding station where bears could come and eat beef fat. After they got used to a human handing out food, Rogers went to the bears and began dispensing the fat in the forest. Typically it took 50 to 100 hours before a bear became completely at ease when Rogers approached it and offered food. At that point, Rogers would stop feeding the bear. He or his assistant, Greg Wilker, would then follow the animal, walking less than 30 feet away from it, taking notes on everything the creature did. The researcher

Electronic collars allow researchers to track a bear's movements and record other data. The collars have been of tremendous importance in the study of wild bears.

would stay with a single bear for up to 48 hours at a stretch. He would eat near the bear and rest when it did; at night, he would doze in a sleeping bag within a few feet of the sleeping bear. Over time, the bear grew accustomed to human-caused noises, such as a cough or sneeze or the sound of a person stumbling or falling down. The scientists followed sows with cubs. They watched bears forage and fight and play. They observed mating. "Males that joined estrous females," commented Rogers, "were the quickest to ignore the inconsequential humans." Never during their research was Rogers or Wilker attacked by a bear.

Among the many observations made by the scientists was that black bears—at least those in the wilds of northern Minnesota—are mainly diurnal: active during the daytime. The bruins go to sleep one to two hours after sunset and slumber until about half an hour before sunrise, a pattern surprisingly similar to that of humans. The same pattern was exhibited by Pennsylvania black bears in a 2004 study by wildlife biologists who used high-tech collars that made a record every second of whether a bear was in motion or at rest. These bears, too, were active during daylight hours and slept through the night. This pattern changed in September and October, when the bears shifted to a nocturnal schedule, perhaps in response to greater numbers of people in the woods during fall hunting seasons.

On a day in August, Wilker watched a sow feed avidly on hazelnuts. The bear searched out fallen nuts on the ground and stole them from the storage middens of red squirrels. The sow used her molars to crack each nut, then chewed it carefully and spat out the hull fragments. During the waking hours of one day, the bear consumed 2,605 hazelnuts (one nut approximately every twenty seconds) with an estimated weight of almost 7 pounds. Rogers watched a bear eat 25,192 tent caterpillars in a day. Over several years of observations, the biologists identified important areas and resources used by bears, and they were able to draw conclusions about social interactions among bears, and between bears and humans. The information collected during the research "is helping forest managers preserve the best bear habitat," Rogers writes, "and is helping campers deal more knowledgeably with bears."

As scientists learn about bears, they are making exciting connections between these large animals and the ecology—and even the landscape—of certain regions.

Charles Robbins of Washington State University studies the physiology and nutrition of grizzlies. He has shown that the great bears shift significant quantities of nutrients from ocean food chains to the land. They do this by consuming salmon, then expelling certain elements as waste in their urine and feces; they also scatter nutrients about when they leave partially eaten salmon carcasses lying on the ground near the rivers and streams up which the fish have swum to spawn. After looking at isotopes of nitrogen and other marine-derived elements, Robbins concluded that some trees in Pacific Rim rain forests grew 60 percent faster than normal because they had been fertilized by salmon-fed grizzlies. Studies farther inland, on Alaska's Kenai Peninsula, suggested that 10 to 25 percent of the growth of trees within a quarter mile of salmon streams was fueled by nitrogen from salmon caught by bears.

Robbins and his colleagues also checked isotopes in museum specimens of bones and fur taken from grizzlies killed in eastern Oregon and central Idaho during the late nineteenth and early twentieth centuries. Up to 80 percent of the major elements in the bones and fur came from the ocean, transported in fish swimming up the Columbia River and its tributaries, before dams stopped the salmon runs and settlers killed off the grizzlies. Like coastal bears, the interior grizzlies, living in dryland sagebrush and prairie habitats, relied heavily on fish. Ecologists believe that the bears' fishing activities and waste products helped promote the growth of riverside vegetation, which in turn provided habitats and food for many other animals, including amphibians, birds, and small mammals. It's hard to gauge the impoverishment of modern riverine habitats in the absence of grizzlies, but it seems certain that those places have become less productive since *Ursus arctos* vanished from the scene.

Science has revealed much about the habits of bears. But many questions remain. Most bears den underground in winter; why do others hibernate on top of the ground, exposed to the elements? What are the details of dispersal, when some—but not all—young bears leave their mothers' ranges to find territories of their own? Why do boars kill the cubs of females living within the males' home areas—some of which could be their own biological offspring? Why do some female grizzlies show altruism by adopting orphaned cubs? What is the exact role of marker trees in ursine social systems?

Another branch of bear science—at once ancient and still in its infancy—involves studying the biochemistry of bears, along with its potential applications in human medicine. As early as the fifth century, the Chinese used bear bile to treat jaundice and abdominal pain and distention, which are symptoms of liver and bile duct problems, including gallstones. When, in the early twentieth century, western scientists analyzed bear bile, they found a component that they named ursodeoxycholic acid (UDCA). Subsequently, medical research revealed that UDCA can dissolve gallstones in humans, relieving the pain, jaundice, and abdominal swelling that they cause. Today UDCA is used in gallstone therapy in many North American hospitals.

Osteoporosis is the thinning of bone tissue. One of its causes is inactivity. People who are paralyzed and patients lying in hospital beds gradually lose bone mass, as do astronauts made weightless when traveling in space. Older people also lose bone tissue, especially if they stop exercising. Studies on hibernating bears have shown that their bones do not thin out, despite a period of inactivity that can last up to half a year. Scientists believe that bears' bodies produce a substance, perhaps circulated in the blood, that maintains bone mass during hibernation. Can this substance be isolated and adapted to treat osteoporosis in our aging population and prevent bone loss in astronauts living in space stations or traveling to distant planets?

As mentioned earlier, hibernation induction trigger (HIT) is a chemical substance that slows down the metabolism of bears and other hibernators.

Injected into monkeys, which do not hibernate, HIT has caused their heart rates and body temperatures to drop, and the monkeys to fall asleep. Organs used in heart, lung, and liver transplants remain viable only for short periods; an American cardiothoracic surgeon found that when organs were treated with HIT, their survival time almost tripled. As scientists learn more about the intricacies of hibernation in bears and other animals, they may be able to apply this knowledge to further extend the life of transplantable organs, thereby saving human lives.

Hunting and Bear Populations

For millennia, people have killed bears for their meat, fat, and fur. Hunting by Native Americans probably had little impact on bear populations: bears have keen senses and are wary and strong, making them difficult prey for hunters armed with bows and arrows, throwing spears, and lances. But, the fact that humans—particularly groups of humans—could sometimes overwhelm bears, including grizzlies, has helped mold ursine behavior in ways that have lasted up to today.

Native Americans regarded bears, especially grizzlies, as prized trophies. Indians of many tribes wore necklaces of bear claws and used hides and parts of bears during religious ceremonies. It was not unusual for Indians to thank a bear for allowing itself to be taken during a hunt and to treat its body, particularly the skull, with reverence. Some tribes wrapped the skull and bones in bark and hung them in a tree or mounted them on a pole. Many Native American legends linked bears with people: often the bears and humans mated, with the offspring of this union conferring great strength and hunting prowess upon the tribe. Some Indians referred to bears in human terms. To the Sauk, the grizzly was Old Man; to the Menominee, he was Elder Brother; and to the Navajo, Fine Young Chief.

When Europeans arrived in North America, they brought with them firearms, steel traps, and the philosophical outlook that the land and its resources had been put there for them to use and exploit. For more than two centuries, many settlers and their descendants hunted and trapped with little regard for seasons or for limiting the take of wild game. People killed a host of wild creatures, including bears, for food and to sell their meat and fur or feathers.

Black Bears

In the East, the new immigrants cleared many thousands of acres of woods, turning the land into fields for growing crops and grazing livestock; they also logged vast tracts of mature forest—formerly excellent black bear habitat—for wood products. A few bears treated the livestock as prey, killing and eating cows, sheep, hogs, and horses. Rarely, a black bear would attack and injure or kill a person. In response to predation by bears, settlers sometimes organized a drive during which a contracting ring of hunters surrounded and shot any predators, including bears, that were caught in the tightening circle. As market killing continued and their habitat disappeared, black bears became scarce, holding on in a few remaining pockets of wild land.

By the late nineteenth to early twentieth century, wildlife had dwindled so alarmingly that conservationists, including many hunters, sought to protect the animals that remained. In the East, newly formed state wildlife agencies took the first steps toward safeguarding and bringing back populations of black bears. Seasons and bag limits were drawn up and enforced. No longer was it legal to shoot bears in the springtime, when, if a mother bear is killed, her young cubs will also perish. In many states, trapping bears was outlawed, and a limit of one bear per hunter per year was enacted. Some states forbade trailing bears with hounds and luring them in with bait, two modes of hunting that are more effective than a lone hunter stalking through the woods with a rifle. Before and while these strictures were put in place, many marginal farms were being abandoned as people moved to cities or headed west to more fertile lands newly opened for homesteading. Over the years, trees reseeded themselves in fields and pastures. Forests returned, and gradually the number of bears began increasing.

A population of bears does not spread out quickly over space, because the females, which give birth to and raise the cubs, rarely disperse very far from where they were born. Bears have often been judged as some of the slowest reproducing animals. It's true that bears do not produce young until they are several years old; generally they do not have large litters; and there is a relatively long interval—two to three years—between litters. But bears live for a long time, and cubs have a high survival rate compared with the young of other mammals. Today most biologists agree that mortality—death caused by hunting, accidents, disease, and other factors—is more of a limiting factor on bear populations than reproduction.

Pennsylvania is a good example of a state where black bears have come back strongly, and today hunting is used there as a management tool to help maintain the population of *Ursus americanus*, minimizing conflicts with humans and keeping bears' numbers in balance with the natural resources on which the animals depend. Hunting also brings in significant revenues, both from the sale of bear-hunting licenses and by hunters' purchases of equipment, food, and lodging. The license revenues benefit other wildlife, including many species that are not hunted.

As early as the 1920s, game wardens in Pennsylvania had begun trapping bears and transferring them to areas where the population had been decimated. Nevertheless, by the late 1960s, fewer than 2,000 bears were believed to inhabit the state. During the 1970s, hunting seasons were closed for three years because of concern over low bear numbers and high kill figures. Biologists with the Pennsylvania Game Commission began an intensive study of the state's bears, radio collaring and monitoring many individual animals. Over the following three decades, data have been collected on more than 53,000 bears, 8,500 of which have been marked with ear tags. Each year, game commission employees capture and immobilize 400 to 600 bears, outfit them with metal ear tags, and release them. Bears have been trapped and relocated to areas with low populations, such as the state's southwestern region, spurring a population expansion. Biologists have designated management units in which the hunting season can be shortened or lengthened if popula-tion numbers warrant it. During the November season, successful hunters must take any bears they have killed to check stations, where technicians interview the hunters and weigh the bears. In the case of untagged bears, the technicians remove a tooth for aging the animal and take other biological sam-ples. Tag returns help biologists monitor the abundance of bears in given areas, the age structure of the population, and the effects of hunting.

As of 2005, Pennsylvania's black bear population was estimated at slightly more than 15,000. In recent years, hunters have killed around 3,000 bruins annually, or roughly 20 percent of the population. In the past, many biologists believed that a population of black bears could sustain a maximum mortality rate of 12 to 18 percent. At least in the rich forested habitats of Pennsylvania, it's clear that a higher mortality rate can be sustained. Ear tag returns have shown that two- and three-year-old bears are twice as likely to be killed as older individuals. Because the season is scheduled for late November, many pregnant females and sows with cubs are already hibernating. Overall, about 23 percent of males and 16 percent of females are removed from the popula-tion each year, with another 2 to 4 percent of bears killed by vehicles. Even with hunters killing so many bears each year, the population of *Ursus ameri-canus* in Pennsylvania continues to rise.

All wildlife populations have a threshold beyond which an overabun-dance of animals begins to harm the habitat, leading to a drop in reproduction and survival. At that point, biologists say that a population is nearing its bio-logical carrying capacity (BCC). Mark Ternent, chief bear biologist for the Pennsylvania Game Commission, writes in *Biology, Status and Management of Black Bear in Pennsylvania* that "the BCC for bears in Pennsylvania is unknown, but there is no evidence that the population is approaching it." Some researchers have suggested that no known black bear population in North America has reached its BCC. In Maine, the population increased from 18,000 in 1990 to 23,000 today, with hunters killing 3,500 to 4,000 bears each year. Biologists believe Maine could support up to 36,000 bears. In general, most wildlife management professionals believe that if bear populations are held at one-half to two-thirds of the BCC, the populations will remain healthy, with bears able to find ample natural foods; not having to compete for those foods, bears will be less likely to venture into human settlements to supple-ment their diets.

As bear populations expand, the likelihood increases that the animals will come into conflict with people. Bears raid beehives and tear apart garbage cans to find food. They kill livestock, particularly poultry and penned rabbits. They eat farmers' crops and break the limbs of orchard trees to get at apples. When crossing highways, bears get hit by cars and trucks, often badly damag-

The incursion of bears into human territory is becoming an increasing problem for wildlife managers.

ing the vehicles and sometimes injuring the human occupants. And occasionally bears hurt people.

At some point, a growing population of bears reaches its social carrying capacity (SCC): the number of animals that the human population will tolerate. Most wildlife agencies try to keep bear populations somewhere near the SCC, which is inevitably lower than the BCC. People thrill to see a bear on an outing in the woods. But they complain when the same bear rips their barbecue unit apart to get at the sweet gunk on the grill, tears their birdfeeder down to eat the seeds, or goes through a screen door to gobble up dog food on a porch. In thinly settled Maine, the state agency in charge of managing wildlife receives an average of 300 bear complaints each year. In Pennsylvania, with more than 11 million people, just one of the state game commission's six administrative regions—the Northeast, centered on the Pocono Mountains, where a burgeoning human population coexists with a healthy population of bears—fielded more than 1,000 complaints during a recent year.

In Pennsylvania, the gradual range expansion of the black bear is putting more bears near towns and suburbs, while more people are simultaneously moving into areas traditionally occupied by bears. To minimize complaints, the game commission works to educate Pennsylvanians not to feed bears or draw them into settled areas; recently a regulation was put in place making it illegal for people to feed wildlife—songbirds included—if the food causes bears to congregate in an area and become habituated to people. The game commission pays for electric fencing to protect beehives and reimburses people who lose hives and livestock to bears. Game wardens trap 200 to 300 problem bears each year and move them to remote sites, even though, reports biologist Ternent, "there are virtually no places left [in the state] with suitable habitat where bears are understocked."

At present, black bears are listed as a game species and hunted in twenty-seven states in the Northeast, South, Upper Midwest, Rocky Mountains, and Pacific Coast. A majority of those states allow hunters to use dogs for trailing bears. Fewer than ten states permit the hunting of bears over bait: increasing

A crowd of visitors to Yellowstone National Park observes some grizzlies from a distance. Though many people delight to see bears under controlled conditions, there is growing friction between bear and human populations elsewhere.

numbers of people believe that baiting gives humans an unfair advantage over game animals. In several states, ballot initiatives have banned both baiting and hounding of bears. Proponents of hunting bears over bait say that the practice lowers the rate of wounding and loss of bears; results in swifter, more humane kills; and allows hunters to avoid killing sows with cubs. The black bear is not hunted in states having small populations of *Ursus americanus*, including Alabama, Connecticut, Florida, Kentucky, Louisiana, Maryland, Mississippi, Missouri, Nevada, Ohio, Oklahoma, South Carolina, and Texas. In some of these states, the black bear is listed as a threatened or endangered species. Black bears are hunted widely across forested regions of Canada, where they remain abundant.

Grizzly Bears

At the time of European settlement, as many as 250,000 grizzlies inhabited western North America, with 50,000 to 100,000 of them living south of Canada. When the Lewis and Clark expedition traveled from St. Louis to the West Coast in 1805, the explorers felt compelled to shoot more than forty-three grizzlies, which they described as "furious and formidable," noting that "it is astonishing to see the wounds [they] will bear before they can be put to death." As furious and formidable as the bears may have been, they were no match for the expedition's single-shot muzzle-loading firearms, and even less so for the breech-loading repeating rifles that soon were invented. By the time a century had passed, up to 90 percent of the grizzlies in the lower forty-eight states had been wiped out—for their meat and fur, to remove them as actual and potential predators of livestock, and to provide peace of mind for the settlers who so feared the big bears. State and local governments paid bounties for dead grizzlies, and federal animal control agents tracked down and eliminated many bears, along with other "vermin," including coyotes, pumas, and wolves. In Canada, grizzlies were slain indiscriminately into the 1950s, many killed with poisoned baits, at a time when little was known about the biology and population of the species there.

By the 1960s, wildlife agencies in both the United States and Canada began to reverse the decades of persecution and neglect. Grizzly hunting still was permitted in Montana, until 1991, when a lawsuit ended that policy. At present, no hunting of grizzlies is allowed in the lower forty-eight states, where *Ursus arctos* is considered a threatened population and receives protection under the federal Endangered Species Act. Grizzly bears currently inhabit five ecosystems in the lower forty-eight states, and the U.S. Fish and Wildlife Service has proposed reintroducing the species to an area in central Idaho.

Although trophy hunting for bears is not looked upon favorably by many people, it continues in Alaska, where around 1,000 grizzlies are legally killed each year, and parts of Canada. Controversy reigns over the actual number of grizzlies in some Canadian provinces and territories; the frequency of illegal and unreported kills; and whether local populations can sustain current harvest rates.

Polar Bears

Of the three North American bears, the polar bear still occupies the greatest percentage of its original range. Its population is thought to have doubled since the 1960s, when the United States, Canada, the former Soviet Union, Greenland, and Norway agreed to strict controls on hunting. The five nations banned hunting bears from aircraft and icebreakers, as had been done in the past. They sponsored research into polar bear populations and behavior, and shared the results of those studies. Today indigenous people in Alaska, Canada, and Greenland are allowed to hunt for the white bears. They shoot around 700 a year and, as they have done for millennia, use the bears' meat, blubber, and hides. Canada has devised a quota system that divides a certain number of permits among the various native communities; native hunters can sell their permits to sport hunters if they wish, providing a source of income for many communities. For the quota system to work properly, scientists must accurately census bear numbers. Critics of the system say that quotas are sometimes set at dangerously high levels.

Poaching

A problem besetting all species of bears is poaching. Russia and the United States share a polar bear population; an international treaty allows hunting by natives of both nations. Conservationists contend that inadequate law enforcement in the Russian Far East has led to widespread poaching, with an estimated 250 polar bears killed illegally in 2002. Also in Russia, many brown bears (the same species as the grizzly of North America) are killed by poachers.

Bear gallbladders are in great demand in several Asian nations, especially China and Korea. The organs and the bile they contain are dried, powdered, and mixed with herbs; the resulting preparations are used to treat various ailments, in health tonics, and as aphrodisiacs. In Vancouver, British Columbia, black-market gallbladders can be bought for $1,000 apiece, then resold in Asia for many times that amount. Most gallbladders come from illegally killed black and grizzly bears. The baculum, or penis bone, of bears is also considered by Asians to have aphrodisiac properties. Bear paws are used to make soup, a single bowl of which can cost more than $800 at a gourmet restaurant in Tokyo. Claws, teeth, and skulls of bears are sold on the black market. Poachers kill bears for their hides and skulls, which are tanned and made into rugs and wall mounts for sale to those who wish to display a trophy.

In parts of Asia, poaching and habitat destruction have pushed several species of bears to the brink of extinction. It's hard to determine how much poaching takes place in North America, but the increasing scarcity of Asian bears is putting additional pressure on American species. Most wildlife specialists agree that poaching is a growing problem, particularly in the western United States and Canada, but also in other parts of the continent, including the Great Smoky Mountains. Some authorities estimate that up to 40,000 black bears are killed illegally in the United States each year. Poachers also take an unknown number of grizzlies in Alaska and Canada. For every bear legally shot by a hunter, it's possible that one or two others die at the hands of poachers.

Bear Attacks

In recent decades, hiking, birding, fishing, foraging, backpacking, and wilderness canoeing have put more and more people into bear country. Human settlements have expanded to include areas frequented by bears, and bears have been drawn to suburbs and rural dwellings, where food sometimes can be more plentiful than in natural settings, particularly in years when crops of wild nuts and berries fail. Each year, people and bears are coming into increasing contact with each other.

Most bears could kill humans easily if they wanted to. But the fact is that bears rarely harm people. Several factors probably account for this restraint. First, both black and grizzly bears had many other, more-powerful carnivores to contend with during the Pleistocene epoch, which ended only around 10,000 years ago, and that situation built a healthy amount of caution into their temperaments. Second, thanks to our sophisticated weaponry, people are deadlier than bears. We have killed so many bears for so many years that a fear of humans has been passed down through the generations, to the point that it likely has become embedded in their genes. And third, by eliminating aggressive bears, humans have selected far more timid ones; to a certain extent, we have molded the bears that exist in subpolar North America today.

When a bear kills a human, the event often becomes national news. Outdoor magazines regularly print photographs and paintings of snarling, slavering bears—usually grizzlies—pandering to people's fears of large predators. Dramatic films play up the potential for mayhem while ignoring the fact that humans and bruins generally coexist. How dangerous are bears, really? How often do they attack humans?

According to Canadian biologist Stephen Herrero, in an introduction to the 2002 revised edition of *Bear Attacks* (a minor best-seller, with more than 82,000 copies sold since it was first published in 1985), bears killed 29 people in the United States and Canada during the 1990s. Of these, grizzlies killed 18; blacks 11. In comparison, every year in the United States, dogs cause the death of around 15 people and injure 800,000 to the extent that they seek medical attention. Statistics show that while engaged in outdoor recreation, a person is much more likely to be struck by lightning than attacked by a bear. And a person is far more apt to be killed in a car accident while traveling to enjoy the outdoors, en route to a trailhead or trout stream, than to run afoul of a bruin. Each year, bears kill an average of 3 people in North America. Each year, more than 15,000 people are murdered in the United States and 44,000 perish in motor vehicle accidents.

Usually when a bear sees, hears, or smells a human, it runs away—fast. Some bears, however, give ground less readily. A bear that has become used to people—through eating garbage, being fed by folks who like to watch bears, or living in an area crisscrossed by hiking trails—is less likely to flee, because experience has taught it that humans are not an immediate, dangerous threat. Some bears learn that by approaching people, they can sometimes get a free meal. A few garbage-eating bears completely lose their fear of humans. They become dangerous animals, ones that may at some point attack a person. Writes Herrero, "In developed areas where black bears have become habituated to human food or garbage, there is evidence of increased danger from females with cubs."

Bears vary in temperament. One bear may be aggressive—toward both bears and humans. Another may be meek and docile. A bear may behave aggressively when it finds itself in a certain condition or situation, such as a sow that believes her cubs are in danger; a ravenous bear that has just killed a prey animal or found a carcass in springtime and begun feeding on it, only to be confronted suddenly by a person; or a bear that has been startled or hemmed in and concludes that it has no escape route.

In general, black bears are much less aggressive than grizzlies. Since they stay mainly in wooded areas, black bears of all ages can usually climb a tree to escape from danger. In contrast, grizzlies evolved as creatures of open terrain, where trees are few or absent; because their claws are straight, they generally

AVERSIVE CONDITIONING

Sometimes called negative reinforcement, aversive conditioning is a relatively new strategy designed to persuade bears that it is unwise—and frightening, and sometimes downright painful—to come too close to human homes, campgrounds, and activities. It can be used on all types of bears. Electric fencing around apiaries or dump areas and pepper spray directed at a bear's eyes and mucous membranes are forms of aversive conditioning. Wildlife technicians employ a variety of additional hazing techniques. They fire guns into the air and shoot "cracker shells" at bears, projectiles that explode loudly above the bruins' heads. They shoot bears in the hindquarters with rubber bullets, which inflicts pain without injuring the animals. Some specialists use Karelian dogs, a breed developed in Finland and Russia to hunt bears and other large animals. The dogs are kept on leashes; they charge at the bears, snarling and barking, accompanied by a team of dog handlers and other humans hollering and shooting off firearms. Even big, dominant grizzlies run from this kind of commotion. If a bear doesn't flee fast enough, the dogs may be let loose to bite at the bruin's heels.

Aversive conditioning works best on young bears and other individuals that have not gotten accustomed to hanging around people's dwellings and feeding on high-calorie foods, such as dog food, birdseed, and garbage. Sometimes it is impossible to permanently scare off bears that have become habituated to people and repeatedly have been rewarded with human-sourced food. In those cases, bears may be captured and then translocated far away from the problem area. Unfortunately, some such bears must be placed in captivity or killed with a lethal injection.

cannot climb trees unless there are conveniently placed, ladderlike limbs. During the Pleistocene, in the grizzly's open, high-plains habitat, females had to be fiercely aggressive to protect their cubs against the many other predators that abounded. Today, when confronted by a potentially dangerous predator—which is probably how most bears view humans—most grizzly sows display that fierceness in defense of their young.

A lot of bears' social behavior amounts to posturing and bluffing. When a bear meets a human, it may behave toward the human as it would toward another bear, particularly if the bear has become habituated to people through feeding on garbage or being fed directly for the humans' entertainment. When a person gets too close to such a bear, the bruin may protect its own personal space by scratching, cuffing, or biting the human—just the sort of behavior it would display toward another bear. That sort of bear-human interaction is particularly apt to take place in a campground where bears have gotten used to being fed by people—and where the bears have pushed things a bit further and begun appropriating people's food. Sometimes bears bluff-charge people to scare the humans away from their food, a behavior akin to one bear chasing another away from a productive berry patch or a carcass.

In a confrontation with a bear that has been habituated to humans, people have two options. They can abandon their food and supplies, which is usually the best option—and the only sane choice to make when the bear is a grizzly. Or, in the case of a marauding black bear, people can advance toward it, yelling or otherwise making a lot of noise; they can throw sticks and stones, trying to persuade the bruin that the food reward is not worth the pain it may have to suffer to obtain those extra calories. Groups of people are more likely than single humans to be able to drive off a bear trying to steal food.

Bears may also bluff humans in other situations, such as when a sow interprets people's presence or actions as a threat to her cubs. Often people wrongly interpret bluff charges as actual attacks, resulting in bears getting shot unnecessarily. Because they are so powerful, bears try to avoid physical clashes with each other, and the same holds true when bears square off against humans. Herrero notes that "an ability to recognize high- and low-intensity threats by black or grizzly bears" may help a person deduce "when a bear is sufficiently agitated that attack may follow if you do the wrong thing." A bear expresses aggression—also called agonistic behavior—in the way it holds its head, how it positions its mouth and ears, whether it moves forward or retreats, and the sounds it makes. Before traveling in bear country, you should study Herrero's excellent book *Bear Attacks*. You also may want to view videos he helped produce, which illustrate specific components of bears' agonistic behaviors and the correct responses to those behaviors. (See the Resources section at the end of this book.)

Attacks on people by bears that are not habituated to humans may be either defensive or predatory. When humans get too close to a female with cubs, the sow may launch a defensive attack. Often such attacks happen when people surprise bear families. If you learn to identify bear habitat and fresh sign, you can stay away from places where bruins are likely to be feeding or resting, minimizing the odds that you will come in contact with a sow and her young. In grizzly areas, to avoid startling the animals, many hikers announce their presence well in advance by talking loudly, singing, or using noisemakers, especially when traveling on trails that curve around slopes or lead through dense vegetation.

If you round a corner and happen upon a bear, watch what the animal does. If it bluffs a charge and then stops, you can probably back away slowly. Do not stare at the bear, because a direct stare is perceived as a threat. Do not run away, as that may trigger a charge. Sometimes you can frighten off a bear by yelling, but the bear may interpret such behavior as aggression and attack. If the bear is a grizzly and a tree is handy, you may be able to climb to a safe height.

If a bear actually attacks you in defense of its cubs or itself, the best tactic is to play dead. Fall on your stomach and clasp your hands behind your head and neck to protect those areas from a damaging bite. (If you are carrying a backpack, it may afford additional protection.) Draw your knees up to your chest to shield your vital organs. Do not move or make a sound, even if the bear bites you or rakes you with its claws. Some hikers have remained so cool during an attack that they have gotten off with injuries no more severe than a few scratches; others have not been so fortunate. In the aftermath of an attack, wait until you are certain that the bear has gone away before moving.

In extremely rare instances, bears attack humans as they would prey. Very few grizzly attacks are predatory in nature; almost all of them are defensive, aimed at keeping the bear safe. In recent years, most, if not all, human deaths and major injuries caused by black bears have resulted from predatory attacks. A black bear living in a remote region may never have seen a human and may look upon a hiker or angler as a potential meal. Some people attacked by predatory black bears have played dead and, as a result, suffered terrible injuries or death. The correct response when attacked by a predatory bear is to fight back. Gouge the bear in the eyes and punch it in the nose. Kick it. Scream at it. If you have an actual or potential weapon, such as a knife or hiking staff, jab it into the bear's face. Try to inflict as much pain as you can.

Many hikers in bear country carry capsaicin spray, derived from extracts of red chili pepper. When pepper spray is shot directly into a bear's eyes, it will usually repel an aggressive or an overly curious bruin. Though it deters both blacks and grizzlies, Herrero points out, "pepper spray is not a substitute for the normal precautions [you should take] when traveling or camping in bear country."

AVOIDING DANGEROUS ENCOUNTERS

Here are some rules to follow that will minimize your chances of having a bad experience with a bear:

- Ask park personnel or local resource managers if bears in the area where you intend to camp or travel have become habituated to humans, and whether "garbage bears" frequent the area.

- When hiking in grizzly country, use binoculars to scan the terrain ahead of you. If you spot a bear, either retreat or carefully detour far downwind of the animal.

- Continually make noises to let hidden bears know that you are approaching. This is especially important in brush and other areas where visibility is limited.

- Travel in a group of four or more people. Grizzlies have been known to attack lone hikers, pairs, and groups of three, but no attack has been documented on four or more humans.

- Do not camp near a game trail.

- Do not camp in an area where bear droppings or tracks are present.

- Avoid campsites that have trash strewn around—good evidence that bears have gotten into the habit of visiting the site to find garbage or steal food.

- Clean any fish well away from camp. If regulations allow it, dispose of entrails by dumping them in high-volume streams or rivers, which can absorb this detritus without becoming polluted.

- Do your cooking at least 100 yards downwind of where you place your tent.

- Store food away from camp, by hanging it in a tree (this may not effectively deter black bears, which are good at climbing), locking it in a bear-proof plastic cylinder, or placing it inside two or three layers of airtight plastic bags and hiding the bags in vegetation.

- Always sleep in a tent. A bear is much less apt to harm a camper inside a tent than one out in the open.

- Learn as much as you can about bear behavior and ecology by reading books and articles. Your goal should be to enjoy yourself and remain at ease in bear country. Keep in mind that your odds of having a bad experience with a bear are very low indeed. If you do encounter a bear, you want to be able to interpret its behavior and react in ways that minimize any danger.

8

Bear Sign

Even if you never see a bear in the wild, you can learn about these intelligent omnivores—and feel their presence in nature—by finding signs of their activities. Based on the evidence at hand, you may be able to deduce what the bear was up to. Biologists refer to this sort of evidence as field sign, while hunters have traditionally called it simply sign. The traces that bears leave in the environment spring from five general categories of ursine behavior: feeding, defecating, resting, traveling, and communicating.

Feeding

Walk along a trail—even a well-used human hiking trail—in bear country, and sooner or later you will probably encounter evidence of bears feeding. Early in the year, before berries ripen and nuts mature, bears eat many insects, particularly grubs, beetles, and ants. Rotten stumps and logs are often broken apart by bruins in search of these insects and their larvae; look for bright, newly exposed yellowish or reddish wood contrasting with the gray, weathered wood that commonly covers logs and stumps. Bears use their powerful shoulders and forelimbs and their claws to get at insect colonies in rotting wood; such colonies occur both in mature forests and in clear-cut areas with abundant slash and stumps. Both black and grizzly bears feed in this manner. You can often find several logs ripped apart in a fairly small area. Pieces of rotten wood several feet away from a log indicate bear work; raccoons and skunks, which also dig for insects in rotten wood, usually do not scatter chips to such a distance.

Check out overturned logs and displaced stones. If you can manage it, push a stone or log back into its original resting place. This may take a fair bit of effort, providing you with a practical demonstration of just how strong a bear is. Claw marks on wood or stone often show where a bear started to pull a log free or dislodge and overturn a stone.

Bears use their paws to scoop open the tops of anthills. They dig out nests of ground wasps, including yellow jackets; look for the nests' gray-brown paper and six-sided honeycombs lying on the ground, in or near the excavation. It can be difficult to distinguish between the workings of raccoons and bears, but holes dug by bears are generally larger and, in areas where wasps are abundant, more numerous. The naturalist Mark Elbroch writes of finding a spot worked over by a black bear, where eight rifled wasp nests were spread over an acre. An earlier naturalist and biologist, Olaus Murie, writes, "In Yellowstone Park I found spots in meadows torn up where a bear had scented an underground ant colony, and in the same park my brother found them turning over buffalo chips for beetles." (Excellent field guides by both Elbroch and Murie will help the amateur naturalist find and interpret sign left by bears and other animals. See the Resources section for details.)

When black bears climb into trees to feed on flowers, leaves, fruit, and nuts, they may leave sign that remains for years. Beech is a common forest tree

in eastern North America, occurring from Nova Scotia south to Florida and west to Wisconsin and Texas. Beech bark is smooth and gray—a perfect surface for recording the claw marks of bruins, which often clamber into beeches to feed on the trees' sweet-tasting nuts. Aspens are also smooth-barked trees; when bears climb into aspens to eat flowers and new foliage in spring, their claw marks show up as black linear scars on the pale greenish gray bark. The scars may persist for the life of the tree, becoming scablike and expanding as the tree's trunk diameter increases. Deep claw marks and broken branches in oak, sassafras, apple, shadbush, and other food-providing species signify the foraging of bears.

Bears use their strength and weight to break down trees with spindly trunks, as well as shrubs such as highbush blueberry

The claw marks of black bears persist for years on smooth-barked trees, like this beech, that bruins climb when feeding on nuts and vegetation.

and autumn olive, giving them better access to fruits, nuts, and berries. You may also find a branch or stem that is not broken but has simply been bent down to ground level by a bruin. In late fall, before black bears enter hibernation, they often search for mast in forested areas; using their paws, they sweep aside the leaves covering the ground to expose fallen nuts. Evidence of this sort of feeding is particularly noticeable after a light snowfall.

Bears bite and pull away strips of outer bark from both hardwood and softwood trees to eat the sweet-tasting inner bark: basswood, pine, spruce, tamarack, and fir are species that bears like to feed on. Look for bark strips lying on the ground at the bases of trees. Vertical gouges from bears' teeth may be visible in the exposed wood tissues.

In the high country of the American West, look for holes where grizzlies have dug out roots, tubers, and ground squirrels. Diggings can be as small and subtle as a single divot, or they can be extensive and prominent—as if, according to Murie, "someone had been sporadically digging a garden plot." Excavations may cover hundreds of square feet. Sometimes a bear rips free and peels back a patch of sod to feed on the roots of grass plants. If hiking in grizzly country, you will want to figure out how recently such an excavation was made: lift up the displaced sod to see whether the vegetation beneath it remains fresh or has become yellow. In habitats edging marine areas in the Pacific Northwest and Alaska, look for places where bears have dug for clams and other shellfish at low tide.

Elbroch claims that "all bears invert carcasses as they feed, pulling the skin over the head, to avoid eating the fur and skin." Bears' prey remains are rarely found—which is fortunate in the case of grizzlies, because a grizzly often will aggressively defend a carcass. In his field guide *Mammal Tracks and Sign*, Elbroch relates a hair-raising tale of a time when he and three companions were participating in a bear-sign survey in Montana's Glacier National Park. While moving down a trail, the humans purposely made noise to alert and frighten off any bears in the vicinity. Their hollering startled a grizzly out of some trailside brush. Although the bear was less than 75 feet away, fortunately it did not charge and instead ran off. The group walked on to discover a black bear that the grizzly had recently killed and had begun feeding on. Elbroch's hastily snapped photograph shows the kill, partially buried with earth and other debris, and with gaping wounds through which internal organs protrude.

A disturbing and all-too-common sign of a feeding bear is an overturned garbage can in a park or campground, its contents scattered about as the bruin searched for something edible in the trash.

Defecating

A significant percentage of what goes into one end of a bear ultimately comes out the other end. Bears process large quantities of food to fuel their large bodies; a black bear will defecate approximately six to eight times per day.

Look for droppings on hiking trails, in wildlife corridors, along logging roads, and in areas where you have found bears' feeding sign.

Biologists have learned much about what bears eat by closely examining their droppings, usually referred to as scats. Wildlife technicians employ forceps and scanning microscopes when studying scats. You don't have to be so systematic; carry along rubber gloves or use a pair of sticks to tease the droppings apart. According to Stephen Herrero in *Bear Attacks*, "Even a superficial examination of the composition of a scat may give you important information." Although he notes that "bear scats seldom smell bad and probably don't contain parasites transmittable to people," Herrero recommends against letting them come in contact with the skin. It's always best to take such precautions. A friend of mine once found a dead black bear carcass decomposing in a small pond in Pennsylvania and retrieved the very large skull, which indicated that the bear had been a mature male. From handling the remains, my friend developed a skin infection that took weeks to clear up.

Bear scats vary greatly in size, diameter, and form, depending on the size of the bear that deposited them and what the bruin had been eating. Cubs leave small scats that may look like the droppings of raccoons. Mature bears have the potential to produce large scats—unless the bear was eating certain types of fruits or animal flesh. Blueberries and strawberries, for example, usually result in a shapeless mass, and meat, including fish, generally produces a dark-colored, amorphous scat. Typical adult black bear scats are 1 1/4 to 2 1/2 inches in diameter and 5 to 12 inches long. Grizzly bears leave scats that are

Bear scat is full of information about foods eaten by the bear that left it. This particular specimen is dotted with red berries.

1¼ to almost 3 inches in diameter and 7 to 20 or more inches long. These figures are approximations, and scats of the two species are difficult and sometimes impossible to tell apart, even by trained technicians.

Bear scats often break up into segments as they are deposited and may show blunt, broken ends. Observers have compared them to horse droppings and human feces, although horse manure usually forms a more copious pile, is lighter in color, and contains smaller plant fragments, and human feces tend to be smaller and less abundant than bear droppings.

The remains of plant items often can be distinguished in bear scats, including grasses, roots, bulbs, nuts, corn, seeds, and fruit pits. Bears are adept at plucking berries from bushes, so you probably won't find many twigs or stems in their droppings. Scats may contain insect remains such as shiny red and black body parts of ants, black-and-yellow wasp parts, or beetle carapaces. Lab technicians regularly find and identify items as small as ant antennae and earthworm bristles. If a bear has been feeding on carrion, its droppings may contain the remains of fly larvae or scavenger beetles. Indigestible parts of prey, such as hair, feathers, claws, teeth, bones, or beaks may show up in scats.

Meat scats usually stink, particularly when fresh. Vegetation scats lack a foul odor. Some foods, such as mushrooms, leave no identifiable traces. Bits of aluminum foil and plastic embedded in dung signify a bear getting into garbage.

Resting

During spring, summer, and fall, black bears may locate their day beds at the bases of substantial, climbable trees, particularly conifers with tall, straight trunks. Mother bears leave their young cubs beneath trees while going off to forage. The cubs rest beneath the trees, which they can quickly climb to escape danger. Vermont tracking expert Susan Morse has dubbed these "baby-sitter trees." Adults' beds show up as oval depressions about 2 feet wide by 3 feet long in leaves, grass, or fallen needles.

Bears also rest out of sight in shrub thickets, including mountain laurel and rhododendron, and in stands of young conifers. Grizzlies loaf among dense willows and alders. Black bears site their day beds on high ground in swamps and on exposed knolls in steep areas. In chilly weather, both black and grizzly bears may build beds. They tear or bite limbs off trees and shrubs and gather them into a pad that elevates the resting bear above the ground; sometimes grasses and conifer boughs are added to the mattress. Along salmon rivers in Alaska, grizzlies rake moss into piles to form beds. A concentration of scats may indicate a bedding area, and bear hairs may be wedged into the bark of nearby trees, against which bears purposely rub.

Bear dens are some of the hardest types of sign to find, but they are among the most exciting to locate. Grizzlies often den on steep, south-facing slopes above timberline. A bear may begin several dens before deciding to complete one and hibernate in it. These "den starts" show up as sizable holes in open terrain, with accompanying fringes or piles of dirt. Grizzlies may begin these digs in early autumn; try scanning for them at this time, using binoculars or a spotting scope.

Entrances to black bear dens vary greatly in size, but many are between 18 and 24 inches tall and approximately as wide. In late autumn, dens may be marked by heaps of newly excavated soil. Black bears are fairly unaggressive animals, but humans still should not go too close to suspected dens at times of the year when the lairs may be occupied. Bears disturbed or startled out of their dens during hibernation burn up calories that their bodies need to survive winter. In summer, when bears are not inside their winter dens, peek into rock crevices and hollows in large logs and at the bases of trees. Look for hairs snagged on rough edges of den entrances. Claw marks may be visible on large trees with cavities partway up their trunks.

Traveling

In moving from place to place, bears leave sign in the form of tracks and trails. As Herrero suggests in *Bear Attacks*, "Seeing bear tracks can be better than actually seeing the bear"—particularly true where grizzlies are concerned. Bears move about on paths, game trails, woods roads, stream banks, and wetlands edges. A good time to look for their sign is a day or two after a rain, when you are most likely to find fresh, sharp examples impressed in mud. Grizzlies and black bears make similar tracks, although there can be noticeable differences between the two species. A simplified description of bear tracks follows; for more information, consult a field guide of animal tracks and sign.

A bear track usually includes three components: toes (with or without marks made by the claws), front pads, and heel pads. The front feet differ somewhat from the back feet and are slightly smaller. When a bear is walking, its back feet often come down directly on top of the prints made by the front feet on the animal's same side. When a bear moves at a rate faster than a walk, its rear feet print ahead of its front feet.

The following information on size and stride of bear tracks is drawn from Mark Elbroch's *Mammal Tracks and Sign*:

In adult black bears, front tracks are $3^3/4$ to 8 inches long by $3^1/4$ to 6 inches wide; rear tracks are $5^3/8$ to $8^7/8$ inches long by $3^1/2$ to 6 inches wide. In grizzlies, front tracks are 7 to $13^1/2$ inches long by 5 to $8^3/4$ inches wide; rear tracks are $8^1/4$ to 14 inches long by $4^5/8$ to $8^1/2$ inches wide. Records exist, however, of grizzly tracks 16 inches long. In black bears, the stride, or distance between tracks, varies from 17 to 25 inches while walking to 24 to 60 inches during a full gallop. Track groups, the area where all four feet print close together, can be as far apart as 75 inches if a bear was galloping. In grizzlies, the stride varies from 19 to 29 inches while walking to 30 to 35 inches at a gallop. Track groups of galloping grizzlies can be 95 inches (almost 8 feet) apart. The trail width—essentially the distance from the outside edges of the left and right tracks—is 6 to 14 inches in blacks and 10 to 20 inches in grizzlies.

In general, grizzlies leave larger tracks than blacks, which can be important to know in areas where both species occur. A female grizzly may leave a track about the same size as that of a male black bear, however.

Bears walk slightly up on their front toes, which often prevents the round heel pad of the front foot from registering. Bears have five toes on each foot, but not all of them may be represented in a track, depending on the firmness of the surface, such as sand, mud, packed dirt, or snow, into which the track was pressed. In bears, the "big toe" is the outer one on each foot, not the inner one as in humans. Sometimes the innermost "little toe" leaves only a faint mark, or no mark at all, making a footprint that appears to be four-toed. In grizzlies, the claws may make small, round holes in the ground well in front of the toe marks. The claw marks of black bears, which have shorter claws, print closer to the ends of the toes.

Both black and grizzly bears have a curious habit of placing their feet in the same spot each time when walking on established trails. This results in a series of shallow pits or worn circles that zigzag down the path. Videos made of bears using such trails show the bruins walking stiff-legged and twisting their feet while in contact with the ground, as if intentionally deepening the trail pattern. Elbroch writes, "Many researchers believe that these trails are a marking behavior, whereby bears leave scent from the glands on their feet and rub it into the earth."

Depending on where it is made, a trail can become quite prominent over time and with repeated use. Traditional bear trails show up dramatically in moss. Grizzlies often create highly visible trails through brush along salmon streams in western Canada and Alaska. Grizzlies wear deep paths into tundra and high mountain areas above the tree line, trails that are often visible from the air. Over the years, a trail may become a pair of parallel furrows, like a miniature wagon trail. Writes Murie, "I have walked in such bear trails but found it awkward, for the brown bear's hips and shoulders are much greater than a man's, and I found it necessary to spraddle widely to keep in the ruts." In wooded terrain, a bear trail often will go under obstructions, such as leaning trees or low branches, that a large grazing animal—an elk, for instance—would be forced to detour around.

Communicating

Bears bite and rub against trees and shrubs to leave social messages. Bears want other bears to read those messages, so they intend for the signposts to be conspicuous. When biologists searched for bear trees in Tennessee, they found them on ridgelines, in valley bottoms, and along game trails, hiking paths, and dirt roads. In Minnesota, researchers located bear trees in forest openings and at the edges of the openings. Both the Tennessee and Minnesota studies were conducted in black bear habitats; in northern and western North America, grizzlies mark trees in similar ways and settings.

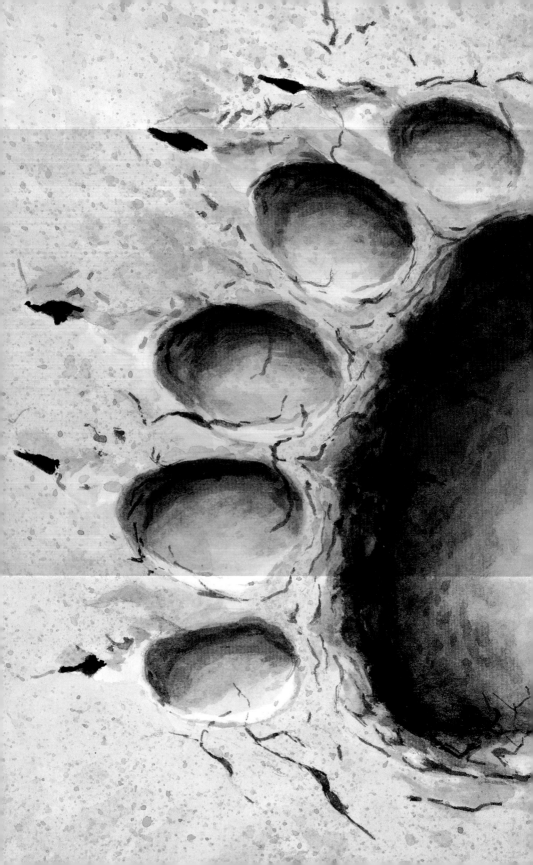

A track from a grizzly's hind foot. Grizzlies' tracks are usually larger than those of black bears, and their claws print farther in front of the toe marks.

In addition to marking trees, bears will also claw and chew human structures such as this post.

A bear tree is very different from a tree that a bear has fed on, climbed into, or scrambled up to find denning shelter or escape danger. Often a bear tree is situated next to a well-used trail, where it can be easily seen. A side trail made by bears visiting the tree may loop off from another, larger trail. Sometimes distinct pits made by bears setting their feet in the same spots, year after year and generation after generation, lead up to a bear tree.

A bear creates a marker tree by taking a bite out of the bark. Most bites are made about 5 feet above the ground (though they can be lower or higher than that) and face a trail or an open area. Over the years, other bears may enlarge the breach. Often a considerable chunk of bark is removed— up to 3 feet in length, in some cases. If the tree is a softwood, it will ooze resin from the gash; if a hardwood, a raised callus may form around the bite as the tree tries to close off the wound with its bark. Look for tooth and claw marks on marker trees.

Bear trees vary in size. Some are only a few inches in diameter, whereas others have trunks several feet wide. Some marker trees end up bitten almost entirely through. When bears girdle trees, the trees will die; spotting a dead or dying tree near a trail can lead you to an old marker tree. Bears also mark utility poles, trail signs, and human structures such as sheds and porch posts.

As they rub their backs, necks, and shoulders against objects, bears often leave fur sticking to resin or hooked into upraised splinters or chips. Bear hair looks like thin human hair; it is not coarse, like the hair of an elk or moose. The hair matches the coat color of the bear, although it may bleach out over time. Grizzly hairs often have silver or white tips.

Bears also use their jaws to snap off saplings and shrubs in travel corridors, feeding habitats, and areas where females are raising cubs, perhaps as a type of communication. Elbroch speculates that bears may also bite trees as a form of displacement behavior that alleviates frustration or sends a warning. Twice he came face-to-face with cornered black bears that had no obvious escape route. "Both bears stood up," he writes, "and repeatedly raked their claws on tree bark, leaving impressive and unmistakable signs while staring me down, vocalizing, and jaw-popping."

RESOURCES

Books

There are hundreds of books about bears. Following are some recent ones and several particularly good or interesting titles.

Bear Attacks: Their Causes and Avoidance, by Stephen Herrero. Guilford, CT: Lyons Press, 2002.

This treatise gives scientific and behavioral reasons for why bears sometimes attack humans. Based on seventeen years of research by the author into bear-human interactions, the book offers information on how to minimize your chances of being attacked and how to react if a bear attacks you. A must for anyone backpacking or camping in bear habitats.

Bears: Monarchs of the Northern Wilderness, by Wayne Lynch. Seattle, WA: Mountaineers, 1993.

This large-format volume provides an overview of what scientists have found out about bears in recent decades, written for a lay audience and illustrated with many excellent photographs. It covers all the bears of the Northern Hemisphere, with a strong emphasis on the three North American species, and includes a comprehensive bibliography citing many scientific papers.

Bears of the World, by Terry Domico. New York, NY: Facts on File, 1988.

A good overview of all the bear species in the world, covering evolution, physiology, intelligence, feeding habits, hibernation, and social behaviors. A large-format book, it includes many photographs.

The Bears of Yellowstone, by Paul Schullery. Boulder, CO: Roberts Rinehart, 1986.

The story of pioneering research into grizzly and black bears conducted in Yellowstone National Park, Wyoming. It includes the natural history of bears and presents a well-written account of bear-human relationships from primitive times to the present.

The Great American Bear, by Jeff Fair. Minocqua, WI: NorthWord Press, 1990.
A natural history of the American black bear, combining accurate science with informative photographs taken by Minnesota bear researcher Lynn Rogers.

The Grizzly Almanac, by Robert H. Busch. Guilford, CT: Lyons Press, 2000.
This natural and cultural history of the grizzly is illustrated with modern and historical photographs, paintings, and etchings.

Polar Bears, by Ian Stirling. Ann Arbor, MI: University of Michigan Press, 1999.
Written by the foremost Canadian polar bear researcher, the book combines accurate scientific information with superb photography.

True Grizz, by Douglas H. Chadwick. San Francisco, CA: Sierra Club Books, 2003.
A highly readable account of grizzly bear ecology, research, and modern aversive-conditioning methods used when bears get too close to humans. Chadwick is a wildlife biologist and nature writer living among grizzlies in western Montana.

Walking with Bears, by Terry D. DeBruyn. Guilford, CT: Lyons Press, 1999.
A bear researcher recounts his work on the Upper Peninsula of Michigan, closely following and observing three generations of black bears.

Field Guides

Mammal Tracks and Sign, by Mark Elbroch. Mechanicsburg, PA: Stackpole Books, 2003.
This is an excellent and extremely thorough guide to mammal tracks and sign. The photographs are many and wonderfully illustrative.

A Field Guide to Animal Tracks, by Olaus J. Murie. Boston: Houghton Mifflin, 1998.
A classic guide to tracks and sign, illustrated with the author's pen-and-ink drawings.

Bear Safety Videos

Biologist Stephen Herrero, author of *Bear Attacks: Their Causes and Avoidance*, helped in the making of the following five videos on bear safety and attacks:

Staying Safe in Bear Country and *Working in Bear Country*, distributed by Magic Lantern Communications Ltd., telephone 800-263-1717, e-mail east@magic lantern.ca.

Bear Attack: The Predatory Black Bear; Bear Attack: Encountering Grizzlies; and *Bear Attack: Polar Bears*, sold by Ellis Vision, Toronto, Canada, telephone 416-924-2186, e-mail sales@ellisent.com.

Helpful Websites

Several of the foundations listed below sponsor courses on bears led by bear biologists. These on-site programs provide an excellent opportunity to safely view and learn about bears. Check the organizations' websites for current offerings.

Churchill Northern Studies Centre
www.churchillmb.net/~cnsc/ab-attracs-bears.html
    The Churchill Northern Studies Centre is an independent research and educational facility located near the town of Churchill, Manitoba, on Hudson Bay. It offers courses about polar bears, including Learning Vacations and Elderhostel "Lords of the North" programs. Nature First Tours and Transportation provides walking-tour services during the prime October–November polar bear viewing season.

Great Bear Foundation
www.greatbear.org
    Based in Missoula, Montana, the Great Bear Foundation is dedicated to the conservation of all eight bear species and their habitats worldwide. It supports research and offers field courses to the general public on black, polar, and grizzly bears. Noted bear researcher Charles Jonkel, a cofounder and president of the foundation, teaches some of the courses.

Interagency Grizzly Bear Committee
www.fs.fed.us
    The Interagency Grizzly Bear Committee was formed in 1983 to work toward the recovery and restoration of grizzly bears in the lower forty-eight United States. The site includes information on bear safety and grizzly bear ecology and science.

International Association for Bear Research and Management (IBA)
www.bearbiology.com
    The IBA is a nonprofit organization working for the conservation of all species of bears. The website includes back issues of *Ursus*, the official scientific journal of the IBA, with abstracts of scholarly papers. It also posts the informative *International Bear News* newsletter, presents information on ordering bear safety videos and applying to visit the McNeil River State Game Sanctuary in Alaska, and gives links to other bear-related sites.

Polar Bears International
www.polarbearsalive.org
    Founded by wildlife photographer Dan Guravich, Polar Bears International is a nonprofit organization dedicated to the conservation of the polar bear. The group funds research into biology and ecology and serves as a central educational resource. The website includes information on the effects on polar bears of climate change, pollution, oil drilling, mining, and hunting; bear attacks; current population status; and conservation issues affecting polar bears.

Wildlife Research Institute

www.bearstudy.org

Working with biologist Lynn Rogers in Ely, Minnesota, the Wildlife Research Institute supports research into black bears and their behavior, and promotes public education concerning bears. The institute offers courses, lectures, field trips, and publications and is working to create the North American Bear Center and an associated museum.

Places to Observe Bears

McNeil River State Game Sanctuary

The sanctuary, in southern Alaska adjacent to Katmai National Park, is managed by the Alaska Department of Fish and Game. People can apply to observe, at close range, grizzly bears feeding on salmon swimming up the McNeil River to spawn during summer. Concentrating on this prolific food source, the bears perceive humans as neutral and nonthreatening. Through a lottery system, interested persons can obtain permits to visit the sanctuary for four-day periods between June 7 and August 25. For information, see www.bearbiology.com/mcneil.html and www.wildlife.alaska.gov/mcneil/index.cfm.

Churchill, Manitoba

On the western shore of Hudson Bay, Churchill is the best place in the world to see and learn about polar bears. This small town draws close to 10,000 visitors a year, all wanting to catch a glimpse of the great white bruins. In addition to the offerings of the Churchill Northern Studies Centre (see the preceding page), other polar bear viewing tours operate out of Churchill, including Tundra Buggy Tours (www.tundrabuggytours.com) and Great White Bear Tours (www.greatwhitebears.com).

Parks, Forests, and Wildlife Refuges

State and national parks, forests, and wildlife refuges are likely places to observe bears and find their sign. Probably your best chance of seeing a bear is in a national or provincial park where they are not hunted and therefore are less afraid of and secretive toward humans. Parks offer ranger-led outings and programs that may deal specifically with bears, and park naturalists can tell you when and where to go to maximize your chances of spotting a bear. Parks with good populations of bears include all of the ones in Alaska, most notably Denali and Katmai; Glacier National Park, Montana; Yellowstone National Park, Wyoming; Yosemite National Park, California; and Great Smoky Mountains National Park, Tennessee and North Carolina. To plan a visit, consult a guidebook such as one of the Sierra Club Guides to the national parks.

In Yellowstone National Park, the most likely time for a visitor to see a grizzly bear is in early spring, just after the bears have emerged from hibernation. At that time, grizzlies move about widely in search of carrion. As Paul Schullery writes in *The Bears of Yellowstone*, "If you can get to the park in April and May, and if the snow will let you drive through, you have the best chance of seeing a grizzly in Yellowstone."

Also by Alan Wolfelt

Healing a Parent's Grieving Heart:
100 Practical Ideas After Your Child Dies

Healing a Child's Grieving Heart:
100 Practical Ideas for Families, Friends, and Caregivers

Healing a Friend's Grieving Heart:
100 Practical Ideas for Helping Someone You Love Through Loss

Healing Your Grieving Heart After Stillbirth:
100 Practical Ideas for Parents and Families

Healing Your Grieving Heart for Kids:
100 Practical Ideas

The Journey Through Grief:
Reflections on Healing

Understanding Your Grief:
Ten Essential Touchstones for Finding Hope and Healing Your Heart

The Wilderness of Grief: Finding Your Way